At the Mind's Limits

JEAN AMÉRY

At the Mind's Limits

CONTEMPLATIONS BY A SURVIVOR
ON AUSCHWITZ AND ITS REALITIES

Translated by
Sidney Rosenfeld and Stella P. Rosenfeld

INDIANA
University Press

Bloomington & Indianapolis

Published in association with
the United States Holocaust
Memorial Museum.

This book is a publication of

Indiana University Press
601 North Morton Street
Bloomington, IN 47404-3797 USA

http://www.indiana.edu/~iupress

Telephone orders 800-842-6796
Fax orders 812-855-7931
Orders by email iuporder@indiana.edu

The paper used in this publication meets the minimum
requirements of American National Standard for Information
Sciences—Permanence of Paper for Printed Library
Materials, ANSI Z39.48-1984.

Manufactured in the United States of America

Library of Congress Cataloging-in-Publication Data

Améry, Jean.
    At the mind's limits.
    Translation of Jenseits von Schuld und Sühne.
    1. Holocaust, Jewish (1939-1945)
—Psychological aspects—Addresses, essays, lectures.
2. Jews—Identity—Addresses, essays, lectures.
3. Améry, Jean—Addresses, essays, lectures.
I. Title.
D810.J4A62213 943.086   80-7682
ISBN 0-253-17724-3 (cloth)
ISBN 0-253-21173-5 (paper)

3 4 5 6 7 08 07 06 05 04 03

Contents

Preface to the Reissue, 1977 / vii

Preface to the First Edition, 1966 / xiii

At the Mind's Limits / 1

Torture / 21

How Much Home Does a Person Need? / 41

Resentments / 62

On the Necessity and
  Impossibility of Being a Jew / 82

Translators' Notes / 102

Afterword by Sidney Rosenfeld / 104

PREFACE TO THE REISSUE, 1977

Between the time this book was written and today, more than thirteen years have passed. They were not good years. One need only follow the reports from Amnesty International to see that in horror this period matches the worst epochs of a history that is as real as it is inimical to reason. Sometimes it seems as though Hitler has gained a posthumous triumph. Invasions, aggressions, torture, destruction of man in his essence. A few indications will suffice: Czechoslovakia 1968, Chile, the forced evacuation of Pnom-Penh, the psychiatric wards of the USSR, the murder squads in Brazil and Argentina, the self unmasking of the Third World states that call themselves "socialist," Ethiopia, Uganda. Given this, what is the good of my attempt to reflect on the *conditio inhumana* of the victims of the Third Reich? Isn't it all outdated? Or is not at least a revision of my text called for?

But when I read through what I wrote at that time, I discover that a revised edition would be nothing but a trick, a journalistic tribute to actuality, that I am unwilling to retract anything I have said here and have but little to add to it. No doubt: whatever abominations we may have experienced still do not offset the fact that between 1933 and 1945 those things of which I speak in my writings took place among the German people, a people of high intelligence, industrial capability, and unequaled cultural wealth—among the people of "Poets and Thinkers." For me this is a fact that until this day remains unclarified and, despite all the diligent historical, psychological, sociological, and political studies that have appeared and will yet appear, at bottom probably cannot be clarified.

All the attempts at clarification, most of which stressed a single cause, failed ridiculously. It is sheer nonsense to speak of a "German national character" or to say that what is contained in the symbolic code words Auschwitz and Treblinka was already in the making in German intellectual history from Luther to Kleist to the "Conservative Revolution" and finally to Heidegger. If one wants to grasp the facts of the matter, it is even less permissible to speak of "Fascism" as the most excessive form of "Late Capitalism." Versailles and the economic crisis with its hardships that drove the people to Nazism is a childish evasion. After 1929 other countries also had their jobless, and among them was America; but it produced a Franklin Delano Roosevelt and not a Hitler. And after Sedan France also suffered its "peace without honor." Certainly, it had its chauvinistic ideologues such as Charles Maurras, but in the front line of its history it had those people who in the Dreyfus case were able to defend the existence of the Republic against the concentrated might of the military caste. No Quisling, no Mussert, no Degrelles, no Sir Oswald Mosley came to power through his people—from the rector of a venerable university down to some poor devil in a big-city hovel, an approving, indeed an exultant people. Yes, the German people exulted when finally the "Day of Potsdam" came, despite the election results that preceded it. I was there. Let no young political scientist, no matter how clever he is, tell me his conceptually untenable stories. To someone who was an eyewitness they appear utterly stupid.

Historiography always sees individual aspects only and misses the forest for the trees, the German forest of the Third Reich. In this case, history itself becomes useless as a concept, and then all that occurs to me is a sentence from Claude Lévi-Strauss's book *La pensée sauvage*, where he says that in the end all historical occurrence dissolves into a chain of purely physical processes, and that the word "history" has no real subject.

On the one hand there is really nothing that provides enlightenment on the eruption of radical Evil in Germany, and on the other hand (despite Chile, despite Brazil, despite the bestial forced evacuation of Pnom-Penh, despite the murder of perhaps a million Indonesian "communists" after the fall of Sukarno, despite Stalin's crimes and the atrocities of the Greek colonels) this Evil really is singular and irreducible in its total inner logic and its accursed rationality. For this reason all of us are still faced with a dark riddle. We know that it did not happen in a developing country, nor as the direct continuation of a tyrannical regime, as in the Soviet Union, nor in the bloody struggle of a revolution fearing for its existence, as in the France of Robespierre. It happened in Germany. It issued, so to speak, through spontaneous generation, from a womb that bore it as a perversion. And all attempts at economic explanations, all the despairing one-dimensional allusions to the fact that German industrial capital, concerned about its privileges, financed Hitler, tell the eyewitness nothing, tell him just as little as the sophisticated speculations about the dialectics of enlightenment.

Therefore, I did not strive for an explicative account at that time, thirteen years ago, and in the same way now too, I can do no more than give testimony. Besides, at this moment I am as little interested in the Third Reich as I was earlier. What occupies me, and what I am qualified to speak about, is the victims of this Reich. I don't want to erect a monument to them, for to be a victim alone is not an honor. I only wanted to describe their condition—which is unchangeable. For this reason I have allowed the text, which was first published in 1966, to stand as it was. Only to the chapter "On the Necessity and Impossibility of Being a Jew" will I make a tiny addition, which for me is gigantic; the present hour demands it.

When I set about writing, and finished, there was no antisemitism in Germany, or more correctly: where it did exist, it did not dare to show itself. People either hushed up the matter of the Jews, or even escaped into an obtrusive philosemitism, which for the respectable victims was an embarrassment, for the less respectable, whose existence must not be concealed, a favorable opportunity to reap good profits from the miserable conscience of the Germans. The tide has turned. Again an old-new antisemitism impudently raises its disgusting head, without arousing indignation—and this, by the way, holds true not only for Germany, but for most of the European countries, with the exception of but a few, such as the upright Netherlands, which shall be very expressly cited here as exemplary. The victims are dying out, it's good that they are, there have been too many of them, for a long time now. The hangmen, too, are croaking—fortunately, and in keeping with the law of biological extinction. But new generations, molded by origin and environment, are constantly rising in both camps, and between them the old unbridgeable chasm is opening again. Someday *time* will close it, that is certain. But it must not be done by hollow, thoughtless, utterly false conciliatoriness, which already now is accelerating the time process. On the contrary: since it is a moral chasm, let it for now remain wide open; this, too, is the reason for the new edition of my book.

It is my concern that the youth of Germany—the ones who are flexible, intrinsically liberal and striving for Utopia, that is, the young people of the Left—do not slip over unawares to those who are their enemies as well as mine. These young people are all too quick to talk about "Fascism." And they don't realize that they are only filtering reality through ill-considered ideologies, that while the reality of the Federal Republic of Germany urgently needs improvement and contains enough shocking injustices—as, for example, the legislation designated as the "Extremists Decree"[1]—that still does not make it fascist.

The FRG is seriously threatened as a liberal polity, just as every democracy always is. That is its risk, its danger, its honor. No one knows better than those who were forced to witness the extinction of German freedom that one must be vigilant. But the chroniclers of the epoch know just as well that vigilance must not change into a paranoid state of mind, which in the end only

works to the advantage of those who would like to throttle democratic free-
doms with their fat butcher's hands. Germany's young leftist democrats, however, have now reached the point where they not only regard their own state
as an already halfway fascist social structure, but in a wholesale manner they
also view, and correspondingly treat, all those countries they designate as "formal" democracies—and among them, above all, the terribly endangered tiny
state of Israel!—as fascist, imperialist, and colonial. For this reason, the time
has come when every contemporary of the Nazi horror must take action—
whatever his action may achieve. The political as well as Jewish Nazi victim,
which I was and am, cannot be silent when under the banner of anti-Zionism
the old, wretched antisemitism ventures forth. The impossibility of being a
Jew becomes the necessity to be one, and that means: a vehemently protesting
Jew. Let this book then, which in a most unnatural way is both untopical and
highly topical, be a witness not only to what *real Fascism* and *singular Nazism*
were, but let it also be an appeal to German youth for introspection. Antisemitism has a very deeply anchored collective-psychological infrastructure,
which in the final analysis can probably be traced back to repressed religious
sentiments and resentments. It can be actualized at any time—and while I was
extremely alarmed, I was really not surprised when I learned that at a rally for
the Palestinians in a large German city not only was "Zionism" (whatever one
may understand by this political term) condemned as a global plague, but also
the agitated young antifascists made their sentiments known through the vig-
orous cry: "Death to the Jewish people."

We are used to that. We had the chance to observe how the word became
flesh and how this incarnated word finally led to heaps of cadavers. Once again
people are playing with the fire that dug a grave in the air for so many. I sound
the fire alarm. I would never have dreamed it when the first edition of my book
appeared in 1966 and I had no other enemies except my natural ones: the
Nazis, old and new, the irrationalists and fascists, the reactionary pack that had
brought death to the world. That today I must stand up against my natural
friends, the young women and men of the Left, is more than overtaxed "dialectics." It is one of those bad farces of world history that make one doubt the
sense of all historical occurrence and in the end despair. The old blockheads
from the ineradicable reactionary camp turn Speer into a German best-selling
author; the young enthusiasts overlook the entire heritage of enlightenment
that is available to them, from the French Encyclopedists to the English economic theorists down to the German intellectuals of the period between the
two World Wars.

Enlightenment. That is a key word. Already more than a decade ago the
present reflections stood, and, so I hope, today still stand in the service of an

enlightenment that can be termed bourgeois as well as socialist. In this context, to be sure, the concept of enlightenment must not be too restricted methodologically, for, as I understand it, it embraces more than just logical deduction and empirical verification, but rather, beyond these two, the will and the ability to speculate phenomenologically, to emphathize, to approach the limits of reason. Only when we fulfill the law of enlightenment and at the same time transcend it do we reach intellectual realms in which *ratio* does not lead to shallow rationalism. This is why, now as well as earlier, I always proceed from the concrete event, but never become lost in it; rather I always take it as an occasion for reflections that extend beyond reasoning and the pleasure in logical argument to areas of thought that lie in an uncertain twilight and will remain therein, no matter how much I strive to attain the clarity necessary in order to lend them contour. However—and in this I must still persist— enlightenment is not the same as clarification. I had no clarity when I was writing this little book, I do not have it today, and I hope that I never will. Clarification would also amount to disposal, settlement of the case, which can then be placed in the files of history. My book is meant to aid in preventing precisely this. For nothing is resolved, no conflict is settled, no remembering has become a mere memory. What happened, happened. But *that* it happened cannot be so easily accepted. I rebel: against my past, against history, and against a present that places the incomprehensible in the cold storage of history and thus falsifies it in a revolting way. Nothing has healed, and what perhaps was already on the point of healing in 1964 is bursting open again as an infected wound. Emotions? For all I care, yes. Where is it decreed that enlightenment must be free of emotion? To me the opposite seems to be true.

Enlightenment can properly fulfill its task only if it sets to work with passion.

Brussels, Winter 1976   Jean Améry

PREFACE TO THE
FIRST EDITION, 1966

When the big Auschwitz trial began in Frankfurt in 1964, I wrote the first essay on my experiences in the Third Reich, after twenty years of silence. At first I did not consider a continuation; I merely wanted to become clear about a special problem: the situation of the intellectual in the concentration camp. But when this essay was completed, I felt that it was impossible to leave it at that. For how had I gotten to Auschwitz? What had taken place before that? What was to happen afterward? What is my situation today?

I cannot say that during the time I was silent I had forgotten or "repressed" the twelve years of German fate, or of my own. For two decades I had been in search of the time that was impossible to lose, only it had been difficult for me to talk about it. Then, however, once a gloomy spell appeared to be broken by the writing of the essay on Auschwitz, suddenly everything demanded telling. That is how this book came about. At the same time, I discovered that while I had contemplated a good many questions, I had not articulated them with nearly enough clarity. Only in the process of writing did I recognize what it was that until then I had indistinctly caught sight of in half-conscious intellectual rumination and that hesitated at the threshold of verbal expression.

Soon the method also asserted itself. If in the first lines of the Auschwitz essay I had still believed that I could remain circumspect and distant and face the reader with refined objectivity, I now saw that this was simply impossible. Where the word "I" was to have been avoided completely, it proved to be the single useful starting point. I had planned a contemplative, essayistic study. What resulted was a personal confession refracted through meditation. I also recognized very quickly how senseless it would be to add still another to the many, in part excellent, documentary works that already exist on my general theme. Confessing and meditating, I arrived at an examination or, if you will, a phenomenological description of the existence of the victim.

Slowly and arduously, I had groped forward in what was familiar to a surfeit, but had remained alien nonetheless. That is why the essays in this book are not arranged according to the chronology of events, but in the order of their writing. To the extent that the reader would venture to join me at all he will have no choice but to accompany me, in the same tempo, through the darkness that I illuminated step by step. In the process, he will come upon contradictions in which I myself got caught up. In the essay on torture, for example, it was still completely unclear to me what significance should be given to the concept of dignity, and I brushed it off with a sweep of the hand, as it were, whereas later, in the essay on my Jewishness, I believed to recognize that dignity is the right to live granted by society. In the same way, while I was writing about Auschwitz and torture I still had not seen clearly enough that my situation is not fully expressed by the concept of the "Nazi victim"; only when I reached the end and pondered on the necessity and impossibility of being a Jew, did I discover myself in the image of the *Jewish* victim.

In these pages, which may be inadequate, but whose honesty I can affirm, much will be said about guilt and also about atonement. For I wished to spare the feelings of others as little as my own. Still, I believe that the findings of this study lie beyond the question of guilt and atonement. I described the state of someone who was overcome, that is all.

I do not address myself in this book to my comrades in fate. They know what it is all about. Each of them must carry the burden of his experience with him in his own way. To the Germans, however, who in their overwhelming majority do not, or no longer, feel affected by the darkest and at the same time most characteristic deeds of the Third Reich, I would like to relate a few things here that until now have perhaps not been revealed to them. Finally, I sometimes hope that this study has met its aims; then it could concern all those who wish to live together as fellow human beings.

Brussels, 1966   Jean Améry

At the Mind's Limits

At the Mind's Limits

TAKE CARE, a well-meaning friend advised me when he heard of my plan to speak on the intellectual in Auschwitz. He emphatically recommended that I deal as little as possible with Auschwitz and as much as possible with the intellectual problems. He said further that I should be discreet and, if at all feasible, avoid including Auschwitz in the title. The public, he felt, was allergic to this geographical, historical, and political term. There were, after all, enough books and documents of every kind on Auschwitz already, and to report on the horrors would not be to relate anything new. I am not certain that my friend is right and for that reason I will hardly be able to follow his advice. I don't have the feeling that as much has been written about Auschwitz as, let's say, about electronic music or the Chamber of Deputies in Bonn. Also, I still wonder whether it perhaps would not be a good idea to introduce certain Auschwitz books into the upper classes of secondary schools as compulsory reading, and in general whether quite a few niceties must not be disregarded if one wants to pursue the history of political ideas. It is true that here I do not want to talk purely about Auschwitz, to give a documentary report, but rather I have determined to talk about the confrontation of Auschwitz and *intellect*. In the process, however, I cannot bypass what one calls the horrors, those occurrences before which, as Brecht once put it, hearts are strong but the nerves are weak. My subject is: At the Mind's Limits. That

1

these limits happen to run alongside the so unpopular horrors is not my fault.

If I want to talk about the intellectual or, as one would have said earlier, about the cultivated man, in Auschwitz, I will first have to define my subject, that same intellectual. Who is, in the sense of the word that I have adopted, an intellectual or a cultivated man? Certainly not every practitioner of a so-called higher profession; advanced formal training is perhaps a necessary condition, but it certainly is not enough in itself. All of us know lawyers, engineers, doctors, probably even scholars who may be intelligent and perhaps even outstanding in their fields, but whom nonetheless one can hardly designate as intellectuals. An intellectual, as I wish to define him here, is a person who lives within what is a spiritual frame of reference in the widest sense. His realm of thought is an essentially humanistic one, that of the liberal arts. He has a well-developed esthetic consciousness. By inclination and ability he tends toward abstract trains of thought. Sequences of ideas from the area of intellectual history occur to him at every occasion. If one asks him, for example, what famous name begins with the syllables "Lilien," he does not think of the glider constructor Otto von Lilienthal but of the poet Detlev von Liliencron. When presented with the cue word "society," he does not take it in its mundane sense, but rather sociologically. The physical process that produces a short circuit does not interest him, but he is well informed about Neidhart von Reuenthal, the courtly poet of village lyrics.

We will take such an intellectual then, a man who can recite great poetry by the stanza, who knows the famous paintings of the Renaissance as well as those of Surrealism, who is familiar with the history of philosophy and of music, and place him in a borderline situation, where he has to confirm the reality and effectiveness of his intellect, or to declare its impotence: in Auschwitz.

Therewith, naturally, I present myself. In a double capacity, as a Jew and as a member of the Belgian resistance movement, besides in Buchenwald, Bergen-Belsen, and still other concentration camps, I also spent a year in Auschwitz, more exactly in the auxiliary camp Auschwitz-Monowitz. For that reason the little word "I" will have to appear here more often than I like, namely wherever I cannot take for granted that others have shared my personal experience.

In the context of our discussion we must first consider the *external* situation of the intellectual, one that moreover was common to everyone else, including the nonintellectuals in the so-called higher professions. It was not a good situation, and it evidenced itself most dramatically in the question of the work assignment, which decided over life and death. The craftsmen in Auschwitz-Monowitz were mostly assigned according to their trades, as long as—for whatever reasons that will not be discussed here—they were not gassed on the spot. A machinist, for example, was a privileged man, since he could be used in the planned IG-Farben factory and had the chance to work in a covered shop that was not exposed to the elements. The same holds true for the electrician, the plumber, the cabinetmaker, or carpenter. A tailor or a shoemaker perhaps had the good luck to land in a room where work was done for the SS. For the bricklayer, the cook, the radio technician, the auto mechanic, there was the slight chance of a bearable work spot and thus of survival.

The situation was different for the inmate who had a higher profession. There awaited him the fate of the businessman, who likewise belonged to the *Lumpenproletariat* of the camp, that is, he was assigned to a labor detail, where one dug dirt, laid cables, and transported sacks of cement or iron crossbeams. In the camp he became an unskilled laborer, who had to do his job in the open—which meant in most cases that the sentence was already passed on him. Certainly, there were also differences. In the camp chosen here as an example, chemists, for instance, were employed in their profession, as was my barracks mate Primo Levi from Turin, who wrote the Auschwitz book *If That Be a Man*. For physicians there was the possibility to find refuge in the so-called sick huts, even if it certainly did not exist for all. The Viennese physician Dr. Viktor Frankl, for example, who today is a world-renowned psychologist, was for years a ditchdigger in Auschwitz-Monowitz. In general, one can say that at the work site the representatives of the higher professions were badly off. That is why many sought to conceal their profession. Whoever possessed even a bit of manual skill and perhaps was able to work with simple tools boldly declared himself a craftsman. To be sure, that meant he was possibly risking his life, namely if it emerged that he had lied. The majority, in any event, tried their luck at playing themselves down. The gymnasium or university professor, when asked about his vocation, timidly said "teacher," in order not to provoke the violent rage of the SS man or the Kapo. The lawyer transformed himself into the plainer bookkeeper, the journalist perhaps passed himself off as a typesetter, in which case there was little danger that he would have to provide proof of his ability at this trade. And so the university professors, lawyers, librarians, economists, and mathematicians dragged rails, pipes, and construction beams. For these tasks they brought with them mostly little skill and but slight bodily strength, and only in rare instances did it take long before they were eliminated from the labor process and ended up in the main camp, where the gas chambers and crematories stood.

If their situation at the work site was difficult, it was no better inside the camp. Camp life demanded above all bodily agility and physical courage that necessarily bordered on brutality. The intelligentsia were only seldom blessed with both, and the moral courage that they often tried to employ in place of the physical was not worth a trifle. Assume for a moment that we had to prevent a professional pickpocket from Warsaw from stealing our shoelaces. Circumstances permitting, an uppercut certainly helped, but by no means that intellectual courage through which perhaps a political journalist endangers his career by printing a displeasing article. Superfluous to say that only very rarely did the lawyer or gymnasium teacher know how to execute an uppercut properly; rather, he was far more often the receiver, and in taking it hardly more able than in giving it. In matters of camp discipline things were also bad. Those who on the outside had practiced a higher profession generally possessed little talent for bedmaking. I recall educated and cultivated comrades who, dripping with sweat, battled every morning with their straw mattress and blankets and still achieved no proper results, so that later, at the work site, they were plagued by the fear—which grew into an obsession—that on their return they would be punished with a beating or the withdrawal of food. They were up to neither bedmaking nor a brisk response to the command "Caps off!" and when the occasion arose, they were totally unable to find that mode of speech vis-à-vis the senior block inmate or the SS man that was both submissive and yet self-assured, and with which threatening danger could possibly be averted. In the camp, therefore, they were as little respected even by higher-ranked prisoners and comrades as they were at the work site by civilian laborers and Kapos.

Still worse: they didn't even find *friends*. For in most cases, it was physically impossible for them spontaneously to use the camp slang, which was the only accepted form of mutual communication. Modern intellectuals quarrel a great deal about their communication difficulties and in the process talk a lot of pure nonsense, which would better remain unsaid. Well, in the camp there truly was a problem of communication between the intellectual and the majority of his comrades. It presented itself hourly in a real and painful way. For the prisoner who was accustomed to a somewhat refined manner of expression, it was possible only with much effort to overcome his distaste for saying "Beat it!" or to address a fellow prisoner exclusively with "Hey, you." Only too well do I recall the physical disgust that regularly seized me when an otherwise quite proper and sociable comrade inevitably found no other form of address for me than "my dear fellow." The intellectual suffered from such expressions as "grub sarge" or "to organize" (which designated the illegal appropriation of some object); yes, even such set phrases as "to go on transport" he uttered only with difficulty and hesitatingly.

But now I have arrived at the basic psychological and existential problems of camp life and at the situation of the intellectual in the narrower sense outlined at the start. Reduced to its most concise form the question that arises is: did intellectual background and an intellectual basic disposition help a camp prisoner in the decisive moments? Did they make survival easier for him? When I put this question to myself I thought first off not of my own day-to-day existence in Auschwitz but of the lovely book of a Dutch friend and comrade in fate, the writer Nico Rost. The book is called *Goethe in Dachau*. I picked it up again after many years and read sentences in it that seemed quite dreamlike to me. For example: "This morning I wanted to go through my notes on Hyperion." Or: "Again read about Maimonides, of his influence on Albertus Magnus, Thomas Aquinas, Duns Scotus." Or: "Today during the air raid warning I tried to think about Herder. . . ." And then, totally surprising for me: "Read still more, study still more, and more intensively. In every free moment! Classical literature as a substitute for Red Cross packages." When I contemplated these sentences and confronted them with my own camp memories, I was deeply ashamed, because I have nothing to compare with Nico Rost's admirable, radically intellectual bearing. No, I definitely would have read nothing about Maimonides, even if—but this was hardly imaginable in Auschwitz—I had come across a book on him. During an air raid warning I certainly would have made no attempt to ponder on Herder. And more despairingly than scornfully

I would have rejected the unreasonable demand that I accept classical literature as a substitute for a food package. As I said, I was much ashamed when I read the book of my comrade from Dachau, until I finally succeeded in exculpating myself somewhat. In doing so, perhaps I did not consider as much that Nico Rost worked in a relatively privileged position as an orderly in a sick barracks (whereas I myself belonged to the anonymous mass of the prisoners) as I did the decisive fact that the Dutchman had been in Dachau, not in Auschwitz. Indeed, it is not simple to find a common denominator for these two camps.

Dachau was one of the first National-Socialist concentration camps and thus had, if you will, a tradition; Auschwitz had been created only in 1940 and to the end was subject to improvisations from day to day. In Dachau the *political* element predominated among the inmates; in Auschwitz, however, by far the great majority of prisoners consisted of totally unpolitical Jews and politically very inconstant Poles. The internal administration of Dachau lay for the most part in the hands of political prisoners; in Auschwitz German professional criminals set the tone. In Dachau there was a camp library; for the ordinary inmate of Auschwitz a book was something hardly still imaginable. In Dachau—as well as in Buchenwald—the prisoners had in principle the possibility to oppose the SS state, the SS structure, with an intellectual structure. That gave the intellect there a *social function*, even if this manifested itself essentially in political, religious, or ideological ways and only in rare cases, as that of Nico Rost, at the same time philosophically and esthetically. In Auschwitz, however, the intellectual person was isolated, thrown back entirely upon himself. Thus the problem of the confrontation of intellect and horror appeared in a more radical form and, if the expression is permitted here, in a *purer* form. In Auschwitz the intellect was nothing more than itself and there was no chance to apply it to a social structure, no matter how insufficient, no matter how concealed it may have been. Thus the intellectual was alone with his intellect, which was nothing other than pure content of consciousness, and there was no social reality that could support and confirm it. The examples that come to mind in this context are in part trivial; in part, however, they must be taken from realms of existence that can scarcely be portrayed.

In the beginning, at least, the intellectual still constantly searched for the possibility to give social expression to his thought. In a conversation with a bunkmate, for instance, who talked at length about his wife's daily menu, he was anxious to slip in the observation that at home he himself had done lots of reading. But when for the thirtieth time he received the answer: "Shit, man!"—he left off. So it was that in Auschwitz everything intellectual gradually took on a doubly new form: on the one hand, psychologically, it became something completely unreal, and on the other hand, to the extent that one defines it in social terms, a kind of forbidden luxury. Sometimes one experienced these new facts at deeper levels than those one can reach during a bunk-bed conversation; then the intellect very abruptly lost its basic quality: its transcendence.

I recall a winter evening when after work we were dragging ourselves, out of step, from the IG-Farben site back into the camp to the accompaniment of the Kapo's unnerving "left, two, three, four," when—for God-knows-what reason—a flag waving in front of a half-finished building caught my eye. "The walls stand speechless and cold, the flags clank in the wind," I muttered to myself in mechanical association. Then I repeated the stanza somewhat louder, listened to the words sound, tried to track the rhythm, and expected that the emotional and mental response that for years this Hölderlin poem had awakened in me would emerge.[2] But nothing happened. The poem no longer transcended reality. There it was and all that remained was objective statement: such and such, and the Kapo roars "left," and the soup was watery, and the flags are clanking in the wind. Perhaps the Hölderlin feeling, encased in psychic humus, would have surfaced if a comrade had been present whose mood would have been somewhat similar and to whom I could have recited the stanza. The worst was that one did not have this comrade; he was not in the work ranks, and where was he in the entire camp? If one ever did succeed in turning him up, then he was so alienated by his own isolation from all things intellectual that he no longer reacted. In this regard I recall my meeting with a well-known philosopher from Paris, who was in the camp. I had learned of his presence and had searched him out in his block, not without effort and risk. We trudged through the camp streets with our tin ration can under our arm, and, to no avail, I attempted to get an intellectual conversation under way. The philosopher from the Sorbonne gave monosyllabic, mechanical answers and finally grew silent entirely. Is the explanation that his senses had become blunted? Definitely not. The man had not become insensitive, no more than I had. He simply no longer believed in the reality of the world of the mind, and he rejected an intellectual word game that here no longer had any social relevance.

A special set of problems in connection with the social function or nonfunction of the intellect arose for the Jewish intellectual of *German educational and cultural background*. No matter to what he turned, it did not belong to him, but to the enemy. Beethoven. But he was being conducted in Berlin by Furtwängler, and Furtwängler was a respected official figure of the Third Reich. On Novalis there were essays in the *Völkische Beobachter* and at times they were not at all that stupid. Nietzsche belonged not only to Hitler, something one could have gotten over, but also to the poet Ernst Bertram, who sympathized with the Nazis; he understood him. From the *Merseburger Zaubersprüche* to Gottfried Benn, from Buxtehude to Richard Strauss, the spiritual and esthetic heritage had passed over into the uncontested and uncontestable ownership of the enemy. A comrade who had once been asked about his profession had foolishly told the truth that he was a Germanist, and that had provoked a murderous outburst of rage from an SS man. In those same days, across the ocean in the USA, Thomas Mann, I believe, said: "Wherever I am is German culture." The German-Jewish Auschwitz prisoner could not have made such a bold assertion, even if by chance he had been a Thomas Mann. He could not claim German culture as his possession, because his claim found no sort of social justification. Among the émigrés a tiny minority was able to constitute itself as German culture, even if there was not exactly a Thomas Mann among them. In Auschwitz, however, the isolated individual had to relinquish all of German culture, including Dürer and Reger, Gryphius and Trakl, to even the lowest SS man.

But also where it was possible to erect the naïve and admissible illusion of the "good" and the "bad" Germany, of the miserable sculptor Thorak, who might be the property of Hitler, and the great Tilman Riemenschneider, with whom one artificially identified—even there, in the end, the intellect had to capitulate unconditionally in the face of reality. For this there are manifold reasons, and it is difficult first to keep them apart and then, as one should, to synthesize them. I will disregard the purely physical ones, although I really don't know if that is permissible, for in the final analysis every camp inmate was certainly subject to the law of his greater or lesser power of physical resistance. In any event, it is clear that the entire question of the effectiveness of the intellect can no longer be raised where the subject, faced directly with death through hunger or exhaustion, is not only de-intellectualized, but in the actual sense of the word dehumanized. The so-called Mussulman, as the camp language termed the prisoner who was giving up and was given up by his comrades, no longer had room in his consciousness for the contrasts good or bad, noble or base, intellectual or unintellectual. He was a staggering corpse, a bundle of physical functions in its last convulsions. As hard as it may be for us to do so, we must exclude him from our considerations. I can proceed only from my own situation, the situation of an inmate who went hungry, but did not starve to death, who was beaten, but not totally destroyed, who had wounds, but not deadly ones, who thus objectively still possessed that substratum on which, in principle, the human spirit can stand and exist. But it always stood on weak legs, and it stood the test badly, that is the whole sad truth. I have already spoken, alludingly, of capitulation or, in other words, of the ineffectual fizzling out of esthetic associations and recollections. In most cases they brought no consolation, at times they appeared as pain or derision; most frequently they trickled away in a feeling of complete indifference.

Now there were, to be sure, exceptions, which arose in certain conditions of mental intoxication. I recall how an orderly from the sick barracks once gave me a plate of sweetened grits, which I greedily devoured and thereby reached a state of extraordinary spiritual euphoria. With deep emotion I thought first of the phenomenon of human kindness. That was joined by the image of the good Joachim Ziemssen from Thomas Mann's *Magic Mountain*. And suddenly my consciousness was chaotically packed to the brim with the content of books, fragments of music I had heard, and—as I could not help but imagine—original philosophic thoughts. A wild longing for things of the spirit took possession of me, accompanied by a penetrating self-pity that brought tears to my eyes. At the same time, in a layer of my consciousness that had remained clear I was fully aware of the pseudoquality of this short-lived mental exaltation. It was a genuine state of intoxication, evoked by physical influences. Subsequent conversations with campmates allow me to conclude that I was by no means the only one who under such conditions briefly attained inner fortification. My fellow sufferers frequently experienced such euphoria too, whether while eating or while enjoying a rare cigarette. Like all intoxications they left behind a dreary, hangover-like feeling of emptiness

and shame. They were thoroughly false and are poor proof of the value
of the spirit. But esthetic notions, and everything that might emerge in
their wake, play only a limited, and not even the most important, role in
the mental life of the intellectual. More essential is analytic thinking; in
the face of terror we might expect it to provide support and direction.

But here, too, I arrive, and arrived, at disappointing results. Not only
was rational-analytic thinking in the camp, and particularly in Auschwitz,
of no help, but it led straight into a tragic dialectic of self-destruction.
What I mean by this is not difficult to explain. First of all, the intellectual
did not so easily acknowledge the unimaginable conditions as a given fact
as did the nonintellectual. Long practice in questioning the phenomena
of everyday reality prevented him from simply adjusting to the realities
of the camp, because these stood in all-too-sharp a contrast to everything
that he had regarded until then as possible and humanly acceptable. As a
free man he always associated only with people who were open to humane
and reasonable argumentation, and he absolutely did not want to comprehend what now truly was not at all complicated: namely, that in regard
to him, the prisoner, the SS was employing a logic of destruction that in
itself operated just as consistently as the logic of life preservation did in
the outside world. You always had to be clean-shaven, but it was strictly
forbidden to possess razor or scissors, and you went to the barber only
once every two weeks. On threat of punishment no button could be missing on the striped inmate suit, but if you lost one at work, which was
unavoidable, there was practically no chance to replace it. You had to be
strong, but you were systematically weakened. Upon entrance to the camp
everything was taken from you, but then you were derided by the robbers
because you owned nothing. The prisoner who was not particularly used
to thinking discriminatingly mostly noted these circumstances with a certain equanimity, the same equanimity that had evidenced itself on the
outside in such assertions as: "There have to be poor people and rich
people" or "There will always be wars." He took note of them, adjusted
to them, and in favorable instances triumphed over them. The intellectual, however, revolted against them in the impotency of abstract thought.
In the beginning the defiant wisdom of folly held true for him: What
surely may not be, cannot be. But only in the beginning.

The rejection of the SS logic, the revolt that turned inward, the
muted murmuring of such incantations as: "But that is not possible," did

not last long. After a certain time there inevitably appeared something that was more than mere resignation and that we may designate as an acceptance not only of the SS logic but also of the SS system of values. And once again the intellectual prisoner had it harder than the unintellectual. For the latter there had never been a universal humane logic, rather only a consistent system of self-preservation. Yes, he had said on the outside: "There must be poor people and rich people," but in the context of this recognition he had fought the battle of the poor against the rich and had not at all perceived it to be a contradiction. For him the camp logic was merely the step-by-step intensification of economic logic, and one opposed this intensification with a useful mixture of resignation and the readiness to defend oneself. The intellectual, however, who after the collapse of his initial inner resistance had recognized that what may not be, very well could be, who experienced the logic of the SS as a reality that proved itself by the hour, now took a few fateful steps further in his thinking. Were not those who were preparing to destroy him in the right, owing to the undeniable fact that they were the stronger ones? Thus, absolute intellectual tolerance and the methodical doubting of the intellectual became factors in his autodestruction. Yes, the SS could carry on just as it did: there are no natural rights, and moral categories come and go like the fashions. A Germany existed that drove Jews and political opponents to their death, since it believed that only in this way could it become a full reality. And what of it? Greek civilization was built on slavery and an Athenian army had run wild on the Island of Melos as had the SS in Ukraine. Countless people had been sacrificed as far back as the light of history reaches, and mankind's eternal progress was only a naïve belief of the nineteenth century anyhow. "Left, two, three, four" was a ritual just like any other. Against the horrors there wasn't much to say. The Via Appia had been lined with crucified slaves and over in Birkenau the stench of cremated human bodies was spreading. One was not Crassus here, but Spartacus, that was all. "Dam up the Rhine with their corpses; piled high with their bones, flow he foaming about the Pfalz"; with these words Kleist poetically addressed the Rhine and, who knows, had he been given the power, he might have translated his cadaver phantasies into reality.[3] A General von Kleist was in command somewhere on the Russian front and perhaps was piling up the corpses of Jews and political commissars. That is the way history was and that is the way it is. One had fallen under its wheel and doffed one's cap when a murderer came along. Once the intellectual's first resistance had flagged, with all his knowledge and analyses he had less with which to oppose his destroyers than the unintellectual. Certainly, the latter stood more stiffly at attention before them and for that reason also pleased them more; for the rest, however, he fought them more spontaneously and effectively through systematic skulking and cleverly executed thefts than did his contemplative comrade.

More than his unintellectual mates the intellectual in the camp was lamed by his historically and sociologically explicable deeper respect for power; in fact, the intellectual always and everywhere has been totally under the sway of power. He was, and is, accustomed to doubt it intellectually, to subject it to his critical analysis, and yet in the same intellectual process to capitulate to it. The capitulation became entirely unavoidable when there was no visible opposition to the hostile force. Although outside gigantic armies might battle the destroyer, in the camp one heard of it only from afar and was really unable to believe it. The power structure of the SS state towered up before the prisoner monstrously and indomitably, a reality that could not be escaped and that therefore finally seemed *reasonable*. No matter what his thinking may have been on the outside, in this sense here he became a Hegelian: in the metallic brillance of its totality the SS state appeared as a state in which the idea was becoming reality.

First a brief personal confession: I entered the prisons and the concentration camps as an agnostic and, on April 15, 1945, freed by the British in Bergen-Belsen, I left the Inferno as an agnostic. At no time could I discover within me the possibility for belief, not even when I lay bound in solitary confinement, knowing that my file was stamped "Troop Demoralization," and for that reason constantly expecting to be hauled off for execution. Also, I was never bound by a particular political ideology, nor was I ever indebted to one. Yet I must confess that I felt, and still feel, great admiration for both my religiously and politically committed comrades. They may have been "intellectual" in the sense we have adopted here, or they may not have been, that was not important. One way or the other, in the decisive moments their political or religious belief was an inestimable help to them, while we sceptical and humanistic intellectuals took recourse, in vain, to our literary, philosophical, and artistic household gods. Whether they were militant Marxists, sectarian Jehovah's Witnesses, or practicing Catholics, whether they were highly educated national economists and theologians or less versed workers and peasants, their belief or their ideology gave them that firm foothold in the world from which they spiritually unhinged the SS state. Under conditions that defy the imagination they conducted Mass, and as Orthodox Jews they fasted on the Day of Atonement although they actually lived the entire year in a condition of raging hunger. They held Marxist discussions on the future of Europe or they simply persevered in saying: the Soviet Union will and must win. They survived better or died with more dignity than their irreligious or unpolitical intellectual comrades, who often were infinitely better educated and more practiced in exact thinking. I still see before me the young Polish priest who had no living language in common with me and who therefore spoke to me in Latin of his faith. "*Voluntas hominis it ad malum*," he said and glanced sorrowfully at a Kapo who was just passing by and who was feared for his brutality. "But God's goodness is immeasurable and thus it will triumph." Our religiously or politically committed comrades were not at all, or only a little, astonished that in the camp the unimaginable became reality. Whoever turned away from God, said the pious Christians and Jews, had to reach the point where he perpetrated or suffered the atrocities of Auschwitz. The Marxists claimed that capitalism, which had entered its final fascist stage, must become a slaughterer of human beings. Here nothing unheard-of occurred, but only what they, the ideologically schooled or God-believing men, had always expected or at least considered possible. Both the Christians and the Marxists, who already on the outside had taken a very subjective view of concrete reality, detached themselves from it here too in a way that was both impressive and dismaying. Their kingdom, in any event, was not the Here and Now, but the Tomorrow and Someplace, the very distant Tomorrow of the Christian, glowing in chiliastic light, or the utopian-worldly Tomorrow of the Marxists. The grip of the horror reality was weaker where from the start reality had been placed in the framework of an unalterable idea. Hunger was not hunger as such, but the necessary consequence of atheism or of capitalistic decay. A beating or death in the gas chamber was the renewed sufferings of the Lord or a natural political martyrdom. The early Christians had suffered that way, and so had the plagued peasants during the German Peasants' Revolt. Every Christian was a Saint Sebastian and every Marxist a Thomas Münzer.

Both Christians and Marxists scorned us sceptic-humanistic intellectuals, the former mildly, the latter impatiently and brusquely. There were hours in the camp when I asked myself if their scorn was not justified. Not that I desired their political or religious belief for myself or that I even would have held this to be possible. I was not in the least bit curious about a religious grace that for me did not exist, or about an ideology whose errors and false conclusions I felt I had seen through. I did not want to be one with my believing comrades, but I would have wished to be like them: unshakable, calm, strong. What I felt to comprehend at that time still appears to me as a certainty: whoever is, in the broadest sense, a believing person, whether his belief be metaphysical or bound to concrete reality, transcends himself. He is not the captive of his individuality; rather he is part of a spiritual continuity that is interrupted nowhere, not even in Auschwitz. He is both more estranged from reality and closer to it than his unbelieving comrade. Further from reality because in his Finalistic attitude he ignores the given contents of material phenomena and fixes his sight on a nearer or more distant future; but he is also closer to reality because for just this reason he does not allow himself to be overwhelmed by the conditions around him and thus he can strongly influence them. For the unbelieving person reality, under adverse circumstances, is a force to which he submits; under favorable ones it is material for analysis. For the believer reality is clay that he molds, a problem that he solves.

That in the camp there could be just as little understanding between the two types, the believers and the nonbelievers, as on the outside, hardly needs to be said. Religious and political comrades paid no attention to us, be it in tolerance, in the willingness to help, or in anger. "You must realize one thing," a practicing Jew once told me, "that here your intelligence and your education are worthless. But I have the certainty that our God will avenge us." A leftist radical German prisoner, who had been thrown into the camps already in 1933, said more pithily: "Now you're sitting here, you bourgeois bullshitters, and tremble in fear of the SS. We don't tremble, and even if we croak miserably here, we still know that after we're gone our comrades are going to line the whole pack of them up against the wall." Both of them transcended themselves and projected themselves into the future. They were no windowless monads; they stood open, wide open onto a world that was not the world of Auschwitz.

The nonbelieving intellectuals were impressed by this bearing, that is certain. Yet I am aware of only extremely few instances of conversion. Only in exceptional cases did the magnificent example of his comrades make a Christian or a Marxist *engagé* of the sceptic-intellectual. Mostly he turned away and said to himself: an admirable and redeeming illusion, but an illusion nonetheless. At times he also rebelled ferociously against his believing comrades' exclusive claim to the truth. To speak of God's boundless mercy appeared outrageous to him, given the presence of a so-called senior camp inmate, a powerfully built German professional criminal who was known to have literally trampled a number of prisoners to death. In the same way, he regarded it as shockingly narrow when the Marxists unswervingly characterized the SS as the police force of the bourgeoisie and the camp as the natural product of capitalism, whereas anyone in his right mind had to see that Auschwitz had nothing to do with capitalism or any other economic system, but that it was the monstrous product of sick minds and perverted souls. One could respect one's believing comrades and still more than once mutter to oneself with a shake of the head: madness, what madness! But the intellectuals fell silent and they found no arguments when the others, as described above, reproached them for the emptiness of their intellectual values. And with that I conclude my digression and return to the role of the intellect in Auschwitz, and repeat clearly what I have already said. if the intellect was not centered around a religious or political belief it was of no help, or of little help. It abandoned us. It constantly vanished from sight whenever those questions were involved that were once called the "ultimate" ones.

What, for example, was the attitude of the intellectual in Auschwitz toward death? A vast, unsurveyable topic, which can be covered here only fleetingly, in double time! I will assume it is known that the camp inmate did not live next door to, but in the same room with death. Death was omnipresent. The selections for the gas chambers took place at regular intervals. For a trifle prisoners were hanged on the roll call grounds, and to the beat of light march music their comrades had to file past the bodies —Eyes right!—that dangled from the gallows. Prisoners died by the score, at the work site, in the infirmary, in the bunker, within the block. I recall times when I climbed heedlessly over piled-up corpses and all of us were too weak or too indifferent even to drag the dead out of the barracks into the open. But as I have said, people have already heard far too much about this; it belongs to the category of the horrors mentioned at the outset, those which I was advised with good intentions not to discuss in detail.

Here and there someone will perhaps object that the front-line soldier was also constantly surrounded by death and that therefore death in the camp actually had no specific character and posed no incomparable questions. Must I even say that the analogy is false? Just as the life of the front-line soldier, however he may have suffered at times, cannot be compared with that of the camp inmate, death in battle and the prisoner's death are two incommensurables. The soldier died the hero's or victim's death, the prisoner that of an animal intended for slaughter. The soldier was driven into the fire, and it is true that his life was not worth much. Still, the state did not order him to die, but to survive. The final duty of the prisoner, however, was death. The decisive difference lay in the fact that the front-line soldier, unlike the camp inmate, was not only the target, but also the *bearer of death*. Figuratively expressed: death was not only the ax that fell upon him, but it was also the sword in his hand. Even while he was suffering death, he was able to inflict it. Death approached him from without, as his fate, but it also forced its way from inside him as his own will. For him death was both a threat and an opportunity, while for the prisoner it assumed the form of a mathematically determined solution: the Final Solution! These were the conditions under which the intellectual collided with death. Death lay before him, and in him the spirit was still stirring; the latter confronted the former and tried—in vain, to say it straight off—to exemplify its dignity.

The first result was always the total collapse of the *esthetic* view of death. What I am saying is familiar. The intellectual, and especially the intellectual of German education and culture, bears this esthetic view of death within him. It was his legacy from the distant past, at the very latest from the time of German romanticism. It can be more or less characterized by the names Novalis, Schopenhauer, Wagner, and Thomas Mann. For death in its literary, philosophic, or musical form there was no place in Auschwitz. No bridge led from death in Auschwitz to *Death in Venice*. Every poetic evocation of death became intolerable, whether it was Hesse's "Dear Brother Death" or that of Rilke, who sang: "Oh Lord, give each his own death." The esthetic view of death had revealed itself to the intellectual as part of an esthetic *mode of life*; where the latter had been all but forgotten, the former was nothing but an elegant trifle. In the

camp no Tristan music accompanied death, only the roaring of the SS
and the Kapos. Since in the social sense the death of a human being was
an occurrence that one merely registered in the so-called Political Section
of the camp with the set phrase "subtraction due to death," it finally lost
so much of its specific content that for the one expecting it, its esthetic
embellishment in a way became a brazen demand and, in regard to his
comrades, an indecent one.

After the esthetic view of death crumbled, the intellectual faced
death defenselessly. If he attempted nonetheless to establish an intellectual and metaphysical relationship to it, he ran up against the reality of the
camp, which doomed such an attempt to failure. How did it work in
practice? To put it briefly and tritely: just like his unintellectual comrade,
the intellectual inmate did not occupy himself with death, but with *dying*.
Then, however, the entire problem was reduced to a number of concrete
considerations. For example, there was once a conversation in the camp
about an SS man who had slit open a prisoner's belly and filled it with
sand. It is obvious that in view of such possibilities one was hardly concerned with whether, or *that*, one had to die, but only with *how* it would
happen. Inmates carried on conversations about how long it probably
takes for the gas in the gas chamber to do its job. One speculated on the
painfulness of death by phenol injections. Were you to wish yourself a
blow to the skull or a slow death through exhaustion in the infirmary? It
was characteristic for the situation of the prisoner in regard to death that
only a few decided to "run to the wire," as one said, that is, to commit
suicide through contact with the highly electrified barbed wire. The wire
was after all a good and rather certain thing, but it was possible that in
the attempt to approach it one would be caught first and thrown into the
bunker, and that led to a more difficult and more painful dying. Dying
was omnipresent, death vanished from sight.

Now of course, no matter where you are, the fear of death is essentially the fear of dying, and Franz Borkenau's claim that the fear of death
is the fear of suffocation holds true also for the camp. For all that, if one
is free it is possible to entertain thoughts of death that at the same time
are not also thoughts of dying, fears of dying. Death in freedom, at least
in principle, can be intellectually detached from dying: socially, by in-
fusing it with thoughts of the family that remains behind, of the profession one leaves, and mentally, through the effort, while still being, to feel

a whiff of Nothingness. It goes without saying that such an attempt leads nowhere, that death's contradiction cannot be resolved. Still, the effort contains its own intrinsic dignity: the free person can assume a certain spiritual posture toward death, because for him death is not totally absorbed into the torment of dying. The free person can venture to the outmost limit of thought, because within him there is still a space, however tiny, that is without fear. For the prisoner, however, death had no sting, not one that hurts, not one that stimulates you to think. Perhaps this explains why the camp inmate—and it applies equally to the intellectual as well as to the unintellectual—did experience agonizing fear of certain kinds of dying, but scarcely an actual fear of death. If I may speak of myself, then let me assert here that I never considered myself to be especially brave and probably also am not. Yet, when they once fetched me from my cell after I already had a few months of punitive camp behind me and the SS man gave me the friendly assurance that now I was to be shot, I accepted it with perfect equanimity. "Now you're afraid, aren't you?" the man—who was just having fun—said to me. "Yes," I answered, but more out of complaisance and in order not to provoke him to acts of brutality by disappointing his expectations. No, we were not afraid of death. I clearly recall how comrades in whose blocks selections for the gas chambers were expected did not talk about it, while with every sign of fear and hope they did talk about the consistency of the soup that was to be dispensed. The reality of the camp triumphed effortlessly over death and over the entire complex of the so-called ultimate questions. Here, too, the mind came up against its limits.

All those problems that one designates according to a linguistic convention as "metaphysical" became meaningless. But it was not apathy that made contemplating them impossible; on the contrary, it was the cruel sharpness of an intellect honed and hardened by camp reality. In addition, the emotional powers were lacking with which, if need be, one could have invested vague philosophic concepts and thereby made them subjectively and psychologically meaningful. Occasionally, perhaps that disquieting magus from Alemannic regions came to mind who said that beings appear to us only in the light of Being, but that man forgot Being by fixing on beings.[4] Well now, Being. But in the camp it was more convincingly apparent than on the outside that beings and the light of Being get you nowhere. You could *be* hungry, *be* tired, *be* sick. To say that one purely and simply *is*, made no sense. And existence *as such*, to top it off, became definitively a totally abstract and thus empty concept. To reach out beyond concrete reality with words became before our very eyes a game that was not only worthless and an impermissible luxury but also mocking and evil. Hourly, the physical world delivered proof that its insufferableness could be coped with only through means inherent in that world. In other words: nowhere else in the world did reality have as much effective power as in the camp, nowhere else was reality so real. In no other place did the attempt to transcend it prove so hopeless and so shoddy. Like the lyric stanza about the silently standing walls and the flags clanking in the wind, the philosophic declarations also lost their transcendency and then and there became in part objective observations, in part dull chatter. Where they still meant something they appeared trivial, and where they were not trivial they no longer meant anything. We didn't require any semantic analysis or logical syntax to recognize this. A glance at the watchtowers, a sniff of burnt fat from the crematories sufficed.

In the camp the intellect in its totality declared itself to be incompetent. As a tool for solving the tasks put to us it admitted defeat. However, and this is a very essential point, it could be used for its *own abolishment*, and that in itself was something. For it was not the case that the intellectual—if he had not already been destroyed physically—had now become unintellectual or incapable of thinking. On the contrary, only rarely did thinking grant itself a respite. But it nullified itself when at almost every step it ran into its uncrossable borders. The axes of its traditional frames of reference then shattered. Beauty: that was an illusion. Knowledge: that turned out to be a game with ideas. Death veiled itself in all its inscrutability.

If we were sitting together and conversing, perhaps someone would ask me what the intellectual actually salvaged from the camp and brought back with him into our world, which we presumptuously call "normal," what spiritual possession he preserved from his time in the camp. I will attempt to answer, to the extent that I have not anticipated the answer already in what I have related.

I will begin with a few negations. We did not become wiser in Auschwitz, if by wisdom one understands positive knowledge of the world. We perceived nothing there that we would not already have been able to perceive on the outside; not a bit of it brought us practical guidance. In the camp, too, we did not become "deeper," if that calamitous depth is at all a definable intellectual quantity. It goes without saying, I believe, that in Auschwitz we did not become better, more human, more humane, and more mature ethically. You do not observe dehumanized man committing his deeds and misdeeds without having all of your notions of inherent human dignity placed in doubt. We emerged from the camp stripped, robbed, emptied out, disoriented—and it was a long time before we were able even to learn the ordinary language of freedom. Still today, incidentally, we speak it with discomfort and without real trust in its validity.

And yet, the time in the camp was not entirely without value for us (and when I say us, I mean the nonreligious and politically independent intellectuals). For we brought with us the certainty that remains ever unshakable, that for the greatest part the intellect is a *ludus* and that we are nothing more—or, better said, before we entered the camp we were nothing more—than *homines ludentes*. With that we lost a good deal of arrogance, of metaphysical conceit, but also quite a bit of our naïve joy in the intellect and what we falsely imagined was the sense of life. In his newest book, *The Words*, Jean-Paul Sartre said at one point that it took him thirty years to rid himself of traditional philosophical idealism. I can guarantee that it did not take us as long. Mostly, a few weeks in camp sufficed to bring about this philosophical disillusionment, for which other, perhaps infinitely more gifted and penetrating minds must struggle a lifetime.

And so I dare to say that we didn't leave Auschwitz wiser and deeper, but we were no doubt smarter. "Profundity has never clarified the world, Clarity looks more profoundly into its depths," Arthur Schnitzler once said. Nowhere was it easier than in the camp, and particularly in Auschwitz, to assimilate this clever thought. If I may quote once more, and once again an Austrian, then I would like to cite the words that Karl Kraus pronounced in the first years of the Third Reich: "The word fell into a sleep, when that world awoke." Certainly, he said that as a defender of this metaphysical "word," while we former camp inmates borrow the formulation from him and repeat it sceptically as an argument against this "word." The word always dies where the claim of some reality is total. It died for us a long time ago. And we were not even left with the feeling that we must regret its departure.

Torture

WHOEVER visits Belgium as a tourist may perhaps chance upon Fort Breendonk, which lies halfway between Brussels and Antwerp. The compound is a fortress from the First World War, and what its fate was at that time I don't know. In the Second World War, during the short eighteen days of resistance by the Belgian army in May 1940, Breendonk was the last headquarters of King Leopold. Then, under German occupation, it became a kind of small concentration camp, a "reception camp," as it was called in the cant of the Third Reich. Today it is a Belgian National Museum.

At first glance, the fortress Breendonk makes a very old, almost historic impression. As it lies there under the eternally rain-gray sky of Flanders, with its grass-covered domes and black-gray walls, it gives the feeling of a melancholy engraving from the 1870s war. One thinks of Gravelotte and Sedan and is convinced that the defeated Emperor Napoleon III, with kepi in hand, will immediately appear in one of the massive, low gates. One must step closer, in order that the fleeting picture from past times be replaced by another, which is more familiar to us. Watchtowers arise along the moat that rings the castle. Barbed-wire fences wrap around them. The copperplate of 1870 is abruptly obscured by horror photos from the world that David Rousset has called "l'Univers Concentrationnaire." The creators of the National Museum

21

have left everything the way it was between 1940 and 1944. Yellowed wall cards: "Whoever goes beyond this point will be shot." The pathetic monument to the resistance movement that was erected in front of the fortress shows a man forced to his knees, but defiantly raising his head with its oddly Slavic lines. This monument would not at all have been necessary to make clear to the visitor *where* he is and *what* is recollected there.

One steps through the main gate and soon finds oneself in a room that in those days was mysteriously called the "business room." A picture of Heinrich Himmler on the wall, a swastika flag spread as a cloth over a long table, a few bare chairs. The business room. Everyone went about his business, and theirs was murder. Then the damp, cellarlike corridors, dimly lit by the same thin and reddishly glowing bulbs as the ones that used to hang there. Prison cells, sealed by inch-thick wooden doors. Again and again one must pass through heavy barred gates before one finally stands in a windowless vault in which various iron implements lie about. From there no scream penetrated to the outside. There I experienced it: torture.

If one speaks about torture, one must take care not to exaggerate. What was inflicted on me in the unspeakable vault in Breendonk was by far not the worst form of torture. No red-hot needles were shoved under my fingernails, nor were any lit cigars extinguished on my bare chest. What did happen to me there I will have to tell about later; it was relatively harmless and it left no conspicuous scars on my body. And yet, twenty-two years after it occurred, on the basis of an experience that in no way probed the entire range of possibilities, I dare to assert that torture is the most horrible event a human being can retain within himself.

But very many people have preserved such things, and the horrible can make no claim to singularity. In most Western countries torture was eliminated as an institution and method at the end of the eighteenth century. And yet, today, two hundred years later, there are still men and women—no one knows how many—who can tell of the torture they underwent. As I am preparing this article, I come across a newspaper page with photos that show members of the South Vietnamese army torturing captured Vietcong rebels. The English novelist Graham Greene wrote a letter about it to the London *Daily Telegraph*, saying:

The strange new feature about the photographs of torture now appearing in the British and American press is that they have been taken with the approval of the torturers and are published over captions that contain no hint of condemnation. They might have come out of a book on insect life. . . . Does this mean that the American authorities sanction torture as a means of interrogation? The photographs certainly are a mark of honesty, a sign that the authorities do not shut their eyes to what is going on, but I wonder if this kind of honesty without conscience is really to be preferred to the old hypocrisy.

Every one of us will ask himself Graham Greene's question. The admission of torture, the boldness—but is it still that?—of coming forward with such photos is explicable only if it is assumed that a revolt of public conscience is no longer to be feared. One could think that this conscience has accustomed itself to the practice of torture. After all, torture was, and is, by no means being practiced only in Vietnam during these decades. I would not like to know what goes on in South African, Angolese, and Congolese prisons. But I do know, and the reader probably has also heard, what went on between 1956 and 1963 in the jails of French Algeria. There is a frighteningly exact and sober book on it, *La question* by Henri Alleg, a work whose circulation was prohibited, the report of an eyewitness who was also personally tortured and who gave evidence of the horror, sparingly and without making a fuss about himself. Around 1960 numerous other books and pamphlets on the subject appeared: the learned criminological treatise by the famous lawyer Alec Mellor, the protest of the publicist Pierre-Henri Simon, the ethical-philosophic investigation of a theologian named Vialatoux. Half the French nation rose up against the torture in Algeria. One cannot say often and emphatically enough that by this the French did honor to themselves. Leftist intellectuals protested. Catholic trade unionists and other Christian laymen warned against the torture, and at the risk of their safety and lives took action against it. Prelates raised their voices, although to our feeling much too gently.

But that was the great and freedom-loving France, which even in those dark days was not entirely robbed of its liberty. From other places the screams penetrated as little into the world as did once my own strange and uncanny howls from the vault of Breendonk. In Hungary there presides a Party First Secretary, of whom it is said that under the regime of one of his predecessors torturers ripped out his fingernails.[5] And where and who are all the others about whom one learned nothing at all, and of whom one will probably never hear anything? Peoples, governments, authorities, names that are known, but which no one says aloud. Somewhere, someone is crying out under torture. Perhaps in this hour, this second.

And how do I come to speak of torture solely in connection with the Third Reich? Because I myself suffered it under the outspread wings of this very bird of prey, of course. But *not only* for that reason; rather, I am convinced, beyond all personal experiences, that torture was not an accidental quality of this Third Reich, but its essence. Now I hear violent objection being raised, and I know that this assertion puts me on dangerous ground. I will try to substantiate it later. First, however, I suppose I must tell what the content of my experiences actually was and what happened in the cellar-damp air of the fortress Breendonk.

In July 1943 I was arrested by the Gestapo. It was a matter of fliers. The group to which I belonged, a small German-speaking organization within the Belgian resistance movement, was spreading anti-Nazi propaganda among the members of the German occupation forces. We produced rather primitive agitation material, with which we imagined we could convince the German soldiers of the terrible madness of Hitler and his war. Today I know, or at least believe to know, that we were aiming our feeble message at deaf ears. I have much reason to assume that the soldiers in field-gray uniform who found our mimeographed papers in front of their barracks clicked their heels and passed them straight on to their superiors, who then, with the same official readiness, in turn notified the security agency. And so the latter rather quickly got onto our trail and raided us. One of the fliers that I was carrying at the time of my arrest bore the message, which was just as succinct as it was propagandistically ineffectual, "Death to the SS bandits and Gestapo hangmen!" Whoever was stopped with such material by the men in leather coats and with drawn pistols could have no illusions of any kind. I also did not allow myself any for a single moment. For, God knows, I regarded myself— wrongly, as I see today—as an old, hardened expert on the system, its men, and its methods. A reader of the *Neue Weltbühne* and the *Neues Tagebuch* in times past, well up on the KZ literature of the German emigration from 1933 on, I believed to anticipate what was in store for me. Already in the first days of the Third Reich I had heard of the cellars of the SA barracks on Berlin's General Pape Street. Soon thereafter I had read what to my knowledge was the first German KZ document, the little book *Oranienburg* by Gerhart Segers. Since that time so many reports by former Gestapo prisoners had reached my ears that I thought there could be nothing new for me in this area. What would take place would then have to be incorporated into the relevant literature, as it were. Prison, interrogation, blows, torture; in the end, most probably death. Thus it was written and thus it would happen. When, after my arrest, a Gestapo man ordered me to step away from the window—for he knew the trick, he said, with your chained hands you tear open the window and leap onto a nearby ledge—I was certainly flattered that he credited me with so much determination and dexterity, but, obeying the order, I politely gestured that it did not come into question. I gave him to understand that I had neither the physical prerequisites nor at all the intention to escape my fate in such an adventurous way. I knew what was coming and they could count on my consent to it. But does one really know? Only in part. "Rien n'arrive ni comme on l'espère, ni comme on le craint," Proust writes somewhere. Nothing really happens as we hope it will, nor as we fear it will. But not because the occurrence, as one says, perhaps "goes beyond the imagination" (it is not a quantitative question), but because it is reality and not phantasy. One can devote an entire life to comparing the imagined and the real, and still never accomplish anything by it. Many things do indeed happen approximately the way they were anticipated in the imagination: Gestapo men in leather coats, pistol pointed at their victim —that is correct, all right. But then, almost amazingly, it dawns on one that the fellows not only have leather coats and pistols, but also faces: not "Gestapo faces" with twisted noses, hypertrophied chins, pockmarks, and knife scars, as might appear in a book, but rather faces like anyone else's. Plain, ordinary faces. And the enormous perception at a later stage, one that destroys all abstractive imagination, makes clear to us how the plain, ordinary faces finally become Gestapo faces after all, and how evil overlays and exceeds banality. For there is no "banality of evil," and Hannah Arendt, who wrote about it in her Eichmann book, knew the enemy of mankind only from hearsay, saw him only through the glass cage.

When an event places the most extreme demands on us, one ought not to speak of banality. For at this point there is no longer any abstraction and never an imaginative power that could even approach its reality. That someone is carried away shackled in an auto is "self-evident" only when you read about it in the newspaper and you rationally tell yourself, just at the moment when you are packing fliers: well of course, and what more? It can and it will happen like that to me someday, too. But the auto is different, and the pressure of the shackles was not felt in advance, and the streets are strange, and although you may previously have walked by the gate of the Gestapo headquarters countless times, it has other perspectives, other ornaments, other ashlars when you cross its threshold as a prisoner. Everything is self-evident, and nothing is self-evident as soon as we are thrust into a reality whose light blinds us and burns us to the bone. What one tends to call "normal life" may coincide with anticipatory imagination and trivial statement. I buy a newspaper and am "a man who buys a newspaper." The act does not differ from the image through which I anticipated it, and I hardly differentiate myself personally from the millions who performed it before me. Because my imagination did not suffice to entirely capture such an event? No, rather because even in direct experience everyday reality is nothing but codified abstraction. Only in rare moments of life do we truly stand face to face with the event and, with it, reality.

It does not have to be something as extreme as torture. Arrest is enough and, if need be, the first blow one receives. "If you talk," the men with the plain, ordinary faces said to me, "then you will be put in the military police prison. If you don't confess, then it's off to Breendonk, and you know what that means." I knew, and I didn't know. In any case, I acted roughly like the man who buys a newspaper, and spoke as planned. I would be most pleased to avoid Breendonk, with which I was quite familiar, and give the evidence desired of me. Except that I unfortunately knew nothing, or almost nothing. Accomplices? I could name only their aliases. Hiding places? But one was led to them only at night, and the exact addresses were never entrusted to us. For these men, however, that was far too familiar twaddle, and it didn't pay them to go into it. They laughed contemptuously. And suddenly I felt—*the first blow.*

In an interrogation, blows have only scant criminological significance. They are tacitly practiced and accepted, a normal measure employed against recalcitrant prisoners who are unwilling to confess. If we are to believe the above-cited lawyer, Alec Mellor, and his book *La Torture,* then blows are applied in more or less heavy doses by almost all police authorities, including those of the Western-democratic countries, with the exception of England and Belgium. In America one speaks of the "third degree" of a police investigation, which supposedly entails something worse than a few punches. France has even found an argot word that nicely plays down a beating by the police. One speaks of the prisoner's "passage à tabac." After the Second World War a high French criminal investigator, in a book intended for his subordinates, still explained in extravagant detail that it would not be possible to forgo physical compulsion at interrogations, "within the bounds of legality."

Mostly, the public does not prove to be finicky when such occurrences in police stations are revealed now and then in the press. At best, there may be an interpellation in Parliament by some leftist-oriented deputy. But then the stories fizzle out; I have never yet heard of a police official who had beaten a prisoner and was not energetically covered by his superior officers. Simple blows, which really are entirely incommensurable with actual torture, may almost never create a far-reaching echo among the public, but for the person who suffers them they are still experiences that leave deep marks—if one wishes not to use up the high-sounding words already and clearly say: enormities. The first blow brings home to the prisoner that he is *helpless*, and thus it already contains in the bud everything that is to come. One may have known about torture and death in the cell, without such knowledge having possessed the hue of life; but upon the first blow they are anticipated as real possibilities, yes, as certainties. They are permitted to punch me in the face, the victim feels in numb surprise and concludes in just as numb certainty: they will do with me what they want. Whoever would rush to the prisoner's aid—a wife, a mother, a brother, or friend—he won't get this far.

Not much is said when someone who has never been beaten makes the ethical and pathetic statement that upon the first blow the prisoner loses his human dignity. I must confess that I don't know exactly what that is: human dignity. One person thinks he loses it when he finds himself in circumstances that make it impossible for him to take a daily bath. Another believes he loses it when he must speak to an official in something other than his native language. In one instance human dignity is bound to a certain physical convenience, in the other to the right of free speech, in still another perhaps to the availability of erotic partners of the same sex. I don't know if the person who is beaten by the police loses human dignity. Yet I am certain that with the very first blow that descends on him he loses something we will perhaps temporarily call "trust in the world." Trust in the world includes all sorts of things: the irrational and logically unjustifiable belief in absolute causality perhaps, or the likewise blind belief in the validity of the inductive inference. But more important as an element of trust in the world, and in our context what is solely relevant, is the certainty that by reason of written or unwritten social contracts the other person will spare me—more precisely stated, that he will respect my physical, and with it also my metaphysical, being. The boundaries of my body are also the boundaries of my self. My skin surface shields me against the external world. If I am to have trust, I must feel on it only what I *want* to feel.

At the first blow, however, this trust in the world breaks down. The other person, *opposite* whom I exist physically in the world and *with* whom I can exist only as long as he does not touch my skin surface as border, forces his own corporeality on me with the first blow. He is on me and thereby destroys me. It is like a rape, a sexual act without the consent of one of the two partners. Certainly, if there is even a minimal prospect of successful resistance, a mechanism is set in motion that enables me to rectify the border violation by the other person. For my part, I can expand in urgent self-defense, objectify my own corporeality, restore the trust in my continued existence. The social contract then has another text and other clauses: an eye for an eye and a tooth for a tooth. You can also regulate your life according to that. You *cannot* do it when it is the other one who knocks out the tooth, sinks the eye into a swollen mass, and you yourself suffer on your body the counter-man that your fellow man became. If no help can be expected, this physical overwhelming by the other then becomes an existential consummation of destruction altogether.

The expectation of help, the certainty of help, is indeed one of the fundamental experiences of human beings, and probably also of animals. This was quite convincingly presented decades ago by old Kropotkin, who spoke of "mutual aid in nature," and by the modern animal behaviorist Lorenz. The expectation of help is as much a constitutional psychic element as is the struggle for existence. Just a moment, the mother says to her child who is moaning from pain, a hot-water bottle, a cup of tea is coming right away, we won't let you suffer so! I'll prescribe you a medicine, the doctor assures, it will help you. Even on the battlefield, the Red Cross ambulances find their way to the wounded man. In almost all situations in life where there is bodily injury there is also the expectation of help; the former is compensated by the latter. But with the first blow from a policeman's fist, against which there can be no defense and which no helping hand will ward off, a part of our life ends and it can never again be revived.

Here it must be added, of course, that the reality of the police blows must first of all be accepted, because the existential fright from the first blow quickly fades and there is still room in the psyche for a number of practical considerations. Even a sudden joyful surprise is felt; for the physical pain is not at all unbearable. The blows that descend on us have above all a subjective spatial and acoustical quality: spatial, insofar as the prisoner who is being struck in the face and on the head has the impression that the room and all the visible objects in it are shifting position by jolts; acoustical, because he believes to hear a dull thundering, which finally submerges in a general roaring. The blow acts as its own anesthetic. A feeling of pain that would be comparable to a violent toothache or the pulsating burning of a festering wound does not emerge. For that reason, the beaten person thinks roughly this: well now, that can be put up with; hit me as much as you want, it will get you nowhere.

It got them nowhere, and they became tired of hitting me. I kept repeating only that I knew nothing, and therefore, as they had threatened, I was presently off, not to the army-administered Brussels prison, but to the "Reception Camp Breendonk," which was controlled by the SS. It would be tempting to pause here and to tell of the auto ride from Brussels to Breendonk through twenty-five kilometers of Flemish countryside, of the wind-bent poplars, which one saw with pleasure, even if the shackles hurt one's wrists. But that would sidetrack us, and we must quickly come to the point. Let me mention only the ceremony of driving through the first gate over the drawbridge. There even the Gestapo men had to present their identification papers to the SS guards, and if, despite all, the prisoner had doubted the seriousness of the situation, here, below the watchtowers and at the sight of the submachine guns, in view of the entrance ritual, which did not lack a certain dark solemnity, he had to recognize that he had arrived at the end of the world.

Very quickly one was taken into the "business room," of which I have already spoken. The business that was conducted here obviously was a flourishing one. Under the picture of Himmler, with his cold eyes behind the pince-nez, men who wore the woven initials SD on the black lapels of their uniforms went in and out, slamming doors and making a racket with their boots. They did not condescend to speak with the arrivals, either the Gestapo men or the prisoners. Very efficiently they merely recorded the information contained on my false identity card and speedily relieved me of my rather inconsiderable possessions. A wallet, cuff links, and my tie were confiscated. A thin gold bracelet aroused derisive attention, and a Flemish SS man, who wanted to appear important, explained to his German comrades that this was the sign of the partisans. Everything was recorded in writing, with the precision befitting the occurrences in a business room. Father Himmler gazed down contentedly onto the flag that covered the rough wooden table, and onto his people. They were dependable.

The moment has come to make good a promise I gave. I must substantiate why, according to my firm conviction, torture was the essence of National Socialism—more accurately stated, why it was precisely in torture that the Third Reich materialized in all the density of its being. That torture was, and is, practiced elsewhere has already been dealt with. Certainly. In Vietnam since 1964. Algeria 1957. Russia probably between 1919 and 1953. In Hungary in 1919 the Whites and the Reds tortured. There was torture in Spanish prisons by the Falangists as well as the Republicans. Torturers were at work in the semifascist Eastern European states of the period between the two World Wars, in Poland, Romania, Yugoslavia. Torture was no invention of National Socialism. But it was its apotheosis. The Hitler vassal did not yet achieve his full identity if he was merely as quick as a weasel, tough as leather, hard as Krupp steel. No Golden Party Badge made of him a fully valid representative of the Führer and his ideology, nor did any Blood Order or Iron Cross. He had to *torture*, destroy, in order to be great in bearing the suffering of others. He had to be capable of handling torture instruments, so that Himmler would assure him his Certificate of Maturity in History; later generations would admire him for having obliterated his feelings of mercy.

Again I hear indignant objection being raised, hear it said that not Hitler embodied torture, but rather something unclear, "totalitarianism." I hear especially the example of Communism being shouted at me. And didn't I myself just say that in the Soviet Union torture was practiced for thirty-four years? And did not already Arthur Koestler ... ? Oh yes, I know, I know. It is impossible to discuss here in detail the political "Operation Bewilderment" of the postwar period, which defined Communism and National Socialism for us as two not even very different manifestations of one and the same thing. Until it came out of our ears, Hitler and Stalin, Auschwitz, Siberia, the Warsaw Ghetto Wall and the Berlin Ulbricht-Wall were named together, like Goethe and Schiller, Klopstock and Wieland.[6] As a hint, allow me to repeat here in my own name and at the risk of being denounced what Thomas Mann once said in a much attacked interview: namely, that no matter how terrible Communism may at times appear, it still symbolizes an idea of man, whereas Hitler-Fascism was not an idea at all, but depravity. Finally, it is undeniable that Communism could de Stalinize itself and that today in the Soviet sphere of influence, if we can place trust in concurring reports, torture is no longer practiced. In Hungary a Party First Secretary can preside who was himself once the victim of Stalinist torture. But who is really able to imagine a de-Hitlerized National Socialism and, as a leading politician of a newly ordered Europe, a Röhm follower who in those days had been dragged through torture? No one can imagine it. It would have been impossible. For National Socialism—which, to be sure, could not claim a single idea, but did possess a whole arsenal of confused, crackbrained notions—was the only political system of this century that up to this point had not only practiced the rule of the antiman, as had other Red and White terror regimes also, but had expressly established it as a principle. It hated the word "humanity" like the pious man hates sin, and that is why it spoke of "sentimental humanitarianism." It exterminated and enslaved. This is evidenced not only by the corpora delicti, but also by a sufficient number of theoretical confirmations. The Nazis tortured, as did others, because by means of torture they wanted to obtain information important for national policy. But in addition they tortured with the good conscience of depravity. They martyred their prisoners for definite purposes, which in each instance were exactly specified. Above all, however, they tortured because they were torturers. They placed torture in their service. But even more fervently they were its servants.

When I recall those past events, I still see before me the man who suddenly stepped into the business room and who seemed to count in

Breendonk. On his field-gray uniform he wore the black lapels of the SS, but he was addressed as "Herr Leutnant." He was small, of stocky figure, and had that fleshy, sanguine face that in terms of popular physiognomy would be called "gruffly good-natured." His voice crackled hoarsely, the accent was colored by Berlin dialect. From his wrist there hung in a leather loop a horsewhip of about a meter in length. But why, really, should I withhold his name, which later became so familiar to me? Perhaps at this very hour he is faring well and feels content with his healthily sunburned self as he drives home from his Sunday excursion. I have no reason not to name him. The Herr Leutnant, who played the role of a torture specialist here, was named Praust. P – R – A – U – S – T. "Now it's coming," he said to me in a rattling and easygoing way. And then he led me through the corridors, which were dimly lit by reddish bulbs and in which barred gates kept opening and slamming shut, to the previously described vault, the bunker. With us were the Gestapo men who had arrested me.

If I finally want to get to the analysis of torture, then unfortunately I cannot spare the reader the objective description of what now took place; I can only try to make it brief. In the bunker there hung from the vaulted ceiling a chain that above ran into a roll. At its bottom end it bore a heavy, broadly curved iron hook. I was led to the instrument. The hook gripped into the shackle that held my hands together behind my back. Then I was raised with the chain until I hung about a meter over the floor. In such a position, or rather, when hanging this way, with your hands behind your back, for a short time you can hold at a half-oblique through muscular force. During these few minutes, when you are already expending your utmost strength, when sweat has already appeared on your forehead and lips, and you are breathing in gasps, you will not answer any questions. Accomplices? Addresses? Meeting places? You hardly hear it. All your life is gathered in a single, limited area of the body, the shoulder joints, and it does not react; for it exhausts itself completely in the expenditure of energy. But this cannot last long, even with people who have a strong physical constitution. As for me, I had to give up rather quickly. And now there was a crackling and splintering in my shoulders that my body has not forgotten until this hour. The balls sprang from their sockets. My own body weight caused luxation; I fell into a void and now hung by my dislocated arms, which had been torn high from behind and were now twisted over my head. Torture, from Latin *torquere*, to twist.

What visual instruction in etymology! At the same time, the blows from the horsewhip showered down on my body, and some of them sliced cleanly through the light summer trousers that I was wearing on this twenty-third of July 1943.

It would be totally senseless to try and describe here the pain that was inflicted on me. Was it "like a red-hot iron in my shoulders," and was another "like a dull wooden stake that had been driven into the back of my head"? One comparison would only stand for the other, and in the end we would be hoaxed by turn on the hopeless merry-go-round of figurative speech. The pain was what it was. Beyond that there is nothing to say. Qualities of feeling are as incomparable as they are indescribable. They mark the limit of the capacity of language to communicate. If someone wanted to impart his physical pain, he would be forced to inflict it and thereby become a torturer himself.

Since the *how* of pain defies communication through language, perhaps I can at least approximately state *what* it was. It contained everything that we already ascertained earlier in regard to a beating by the police: the border violation of my self by the other, which can be neither neutralized by the expectation of help nor rectified through resistance. Torture is all that, but in addition very much more. Whoever is overcome by pain through torture experiences his body as never before. In self-negation, his flesh becomes a total reality. Partially, torture is one of those life experiences that in a milder form present themselves also to the consciousness of the patient who is awaiting help, and the popular saying according to which we feel well as long as we do not feel our body does indeed express an undeniable truth. But only in torture does the transformation of the person into flesh become complete. Frail in the face of violence, yelling out in pain, awaiting no help, capable of no resistance, the tortured person is only a body, and nothing else beside that. If what Thomas Mann described years ago in *The Magic Mountain* is true, namely, that the more hopelessly man's body is subjected to suffering, the more physical he is, then of all physical celebrations torture is the most terrible. In the case of Mann's consumptives, they still took place in a state of euphoria; for the martyred they are death rituals.

It is tempting to speculate further. Pain, we said, is the most extreme intensification imaginable of our bodily being. But maybe it is even more, that is: death. No road that can be travelled by logic leads us to death, but perhaps the thought is permissible that through pain a path of feeling and premonition can be paved to it for us. In the end, we would be faced with the equation: Body = Pain = Death, and in our case this could be reduced to the hypothesis that torture, through which we are turned into body by the other, blots out the contradiction of death and allows us to experience it personally. But this is an evasion of the question. We have for it only the excuse of our own experience and must add in explanation that torture has an indelible character. Whoever was tortured, stays tortured. Torture is ineradicably burned into him, even when no clinically objective traces can be detected. The permanence of torture gives the one who underwent it the right to speculative flights, which need not be lofty ones and still may claim a certain validity.

I speak of the martyred. But it is time to say something about the tormentors also. No bridge leads from the former to the latter. Modern police torture is without the theological complicity that, no doubt, in the Inquisition joined both sides; faith united them even in the delight of tormenting and the pain of being tormented. The torturer believed he was exercising God's justice, since he was, after all, purifying the offender's soul; the tortured heretic or witch did not at all deny him this right. There was a horrible and perverted togetherness. In present-day torture not a bit of this remains. For the tortured, the torturer is solely the other, and here he will be regarded as such.

Who were the others, who pulled me up by my dislocated arms and punished my dangling body with the horsewhip? As a start, one can take the view that they were merely brutalized petty bourgeois and subordinate bureaucrats of torture. But it is necessary to abandon this point of view immediately if one wishes to arrive at an insight into evil that is more than just banal. Were they sadists, then? According to my well-founded conviction, they were not sadists in the narrow sexual-pathologic sense. In general, I don't believe that I encountered a single genuine sadist of this sort during my two years of imprisonment by the Gestapo and in concentration camps. But probably they *were* sadists if we leave sexual pathology aside and attempt to judge the torturers according to the categories of, well, the *philosophy* of the Marquis de Sade. Sadism as the dis-ordered view of the world is something other than the sadism of the usual psychology handbooks, also other than the sadism interpretation of Freudian analysis. For this reason, the French anthropologist Georges

Bataille will be cited here, who has reflected very thoroughly on the odd Marquis. We will then perhaps see not only that my tormentors lived on the border of a sadistic philosophy but that National Socialism in its totality was stamped less with the seal of a hardly definable "totalitarianism" than with that of *sadism*.

For Georges Bataille, sadism is to be understood not in the light of sexual pathology but rather in that of existential psychology, in which it appears as the radical negation of the other, as the denial of the social principle as well as the reality principle. A world in which torture, destruction, and death triumph obviously cannot exist. But the sadist does not care about the continued existence of the world. On the contrary, he wants to nullify this world, and by negating his fellow man, who also in an entirely specific sense is "hell" for him, he wants to realize his own total sovereignty. The fellow man is transformed into flesh, and in this transformation he is already brought to the edge of death; if worst comes to worst, he is driven beyond the border of death into Nothingness. With that the torturer and murderer realizes his own destructive being, without having to lose himself in it entirely, like his martyred victim. He can, after all, cease the torture when it suits him. He has control of the other's scream of pain and death; he is master over flesh and spirit, life and death. In this way, torture becomes the total inversion of the social world, in which we can live only if we grant our fellow man life, ease his suffering, bridle the desire of our ego to expand. But in the world of torture man exists only by ruining the other person who stands before him. A slight pressure by the tool-wielding hand is enough to turn the other—along with his head, in which are perhaps stored Kant and Hegel, and all nine symphonies, and the World as Will and Representation—into a shrilly squealing piglet at slaughter. When it has happened and the torturer has expanded into the body of his fellow man and extinguished what was his spirit, he himself can then smoke a cigarette or sit down to breakfast or, if he has the desire, have a look in at the World as Will and Representation.

My boys at Breendonk contented themselves with the cigarette and, as soon as they were tired of torturing, doubtlessly let old Schopenhauer be. But this still does not mean that the evil they inflicted on me was banal. If one insists on it, they were bureaucrats of torture. And yet, they were also much more. I saw it in their serious, tense faces, which were not

swelling, let us say, with sexual-sadistic delight, but concentrated in murderous self-realization. With heart and soul they went about their business, and the name of it was power, dominion over spirit and flesh, orgy
of unchecked self-expansion. I also have not forgotten that there were
moments when I felt a kind of wretched admiration for the agonizing
sovereignty they exercised over me. For is not the one who can reduce a
person so entirely to a body and a whimpering prey of death a god or, at
least, a demigod?

But the concentrated effort of torture naturally did not make these
people forget their profession. They were "cops," that was métier and
routine. And so they continued asking me questions, constantly the same
ones: accomplices, addresses, meeting places. To come right out with it:
I had nothing but luck, because especially in regard to the extorting of
information our group was rather well organized. What they wanted to
hear from me in Breendonk, I simply did not know myself. If instead of
the aliases I had been able to name the real names, perhaps, or probably,
a calamity would have occurred, and I would be standing here now as
the weakling I most likely am, and as the traitor I potentially already was.
Yet it was not at all that I opposed them with the heroically maintained
silence that befits a real man in such a situation and about which one may
read (almost always, incidentally, in reports by people who were not there
themselves). I talked. I accused myself of invented absurd political crimes,
and even now I don't know at all how they could have occurred to me,
dangling bundle that I was. Apparently I had the hope that, after such
incriminating disclosures, a well-aimed blow to the head would put an
end to my misery and quickly bring on my death, or at least unconscious-
ness. Finally, I actually did become unconscious, and with that it was over
for a while—for the "cops" abstained from awakening their battered victim, since the nonsense I had foisted on them was busying their stupid
heads.

It was over for a while. It still is not over. Twenty-two years later I am
still dangling over the ground by dislocated arms, panting, and accusing
myself. In such an instance there is no "repression." Does one repress an
unsightly birthmark? One can have it removed by a plastic surgeon, but
the skin that is transplanted in its place is not the skin with which one
feels naturally at ease.

One can shake off torture as little as the question of the possibilities

and limits of the power to resist it. I have spoken with many comrades
about this and have attempted to relive all kinds of experiences. Does the
brave man resist? I am not sure. There was, for example, that young
Belgian aristocrat who converted to Communism and was something like
a hero, namely in the Spanish civil war, where he had fought on the
Republican side. But when they subjected him to torture in Breendonk,
he "coughed up," as it is put in the jargon of common criminals, and
since he knew a lot, he betrayed an entire organization. The brave man
went very far in his readiness to cooperate. He drove with the Gestapo
men to the homes of his comrades and in extreme zeal encouraged them
to confess just everything, but absolutely everything, that was their only
hope, and it was, he said, a question of paying any price in order to escape
torture. And I knew another, a Bulgarian professional revolutionary, who
had been subjected to torture compared to which mine was only a somewhat strenuous sport, and who had remained silent, simply and stead-
fastly silent. Also the unforgettable Jean Moulin, who is buried in the
Pantheon in Paris, shall be remembered here. He was arrested as the first
chairman of the French Resistance Movement. If he had talked, the entire
Résistance would have been destroyed. But he bore his martyrdom beyond
the limits of death and did not betray one single name.

Where does the strength, where does the weakness come from? I don't
know. One does not know. No one has yet been able to draw distinct
borders between the "moral" power of resistance to physical pain and
"bodily" resistance (which likewise must be placed in quotation marks).
There are more than a few specialists who reduce the entire problem of
bearing pain to a purely physiological basis. Here only the French professor of surgery and member of the Collège de France, René Leriche, will
be cited, who ventured the following judgment:

"We are not equal before the phenomenon of pain," the professor says.

One person already suffers where the other apparently still perceives
hardly anything. This has to do with the individual quality of our sym-
pathetic nerve, with the hormone of the parathyroid gland, and with the
vasoconstrictive substances of the adrenal glands. Also in the physiological observation of pain we cannot escape the concept of individuality.
History shows us that we people of today are more sensitive to pain than
our ancestors were, and this from a purely physiological standpoint. I am
not speaking here of any hypothetical moral power of resistance, but am
staying within the realm of physiology. Pain remedies and narcosis have

contributed more to our greater sensitivity than moral factors. Also the reactions to pain by various people are absolutely not the same. Two wars have given us the opportunity to see how the physical sensitivities of the Germans, French, and English differ. Above all, there is a great separation in this regard between the Europeans on the one hand and the Asians and Africans on the other. The latter bear physical pain incomparably better than the former . . .

Thus the judgment of a surgical authority. It will hardly be disputed by the simple experiences of a nonprofessional, who saw many individuals and members of numerous ethnic groups suffering pain and deprivation. In this connection, it occurs to me that, as I was able to observe later in the concentration camp, the Slavs, and especially the Russians, bore physical injustice easier and more stoically than did, for example, Italians, Frenchmen, Hollanders, or Scandinavians. As body, we actually are not equal when faced with pain and torture. But that does not solve our problem of the power of resistance, and it gives us no conclusive answer to the question of what share moral and physical factors have in it. If we agree to a reduction to the purely physiological, then we run the risk of finally pardoning every kind of whiny reaction and physical cowardice. But if we exclusively stress the so-called moral resistance, then we would have to measure a weakly seventeen-year-old gymnasium pupil who fails to withstand torture by the same standards as an athletically built thirty-year-old laborer who is accustomed to manual work and hardships. Thus we had better let the question rest, just as at that time I myself did not further analyze my power to resist, when, battered and with my hands still shackled, I lay in the cell and ruminated.

For the person who has survived torture and whose pains are starting to subside (before they flare up again) experiences an ephemeral peace that is conducive to thinking. In one respect, the tortured person is content that he was body only and because of that, so he thinks, free of all political concern. You are on the outside, he tells himself more or less, and I am here in the cell, and that gives me a great superiority over you. I have experienced the ineffable, I am filled with it entirely, and now see, if you can, how you are going to live with yourselves, the world, and my disappearance. On the other hand, however, the fading away of the physical, which revealed itself in pain and torture, the end of the tremendous tumult that had erupted in the body, the reattainment of a hollow stability, is satisfying and soothing. There are even euphoric moments, in which the return of weak powers of reason is felt as an extraordinary happiness. The bundle of limbs that is slowly recovering human semblance feels the urge to articulate the experience intellectually, right away, on the spot, without losing the least bit of time, for a few hours afterward could already be too late.

Thinking is almost nothing else but a great astonishment. Astonishment at the fact that you had endured it, that the tumult had not immediately led also to an explosion of the body, that you still have a forehead that you can stroke with your shackled hands, an eye that can be opened and closed, a mouth that would show the usual lines if you could see it now in a mirror. What? you ask yourself—the same person who was gruff with his family because of a toothache was able to hang there by his dislocated arms and still live? The person who for hours was in a bad mood after slightly burning his finger with a cigarette was lacerated here with a horsewhip, and now that it is all over he hardly feels his wounds? Astonishment also at the fact that what happened to you yourself, by right was supposed to befall only those who had written about it in accusatory brochures: torture. A murder is committed, but it is part of the newspaper that reported on it. An airplane accident occurred, but that concerns the people who lost a relative in it. The Gestapo tortures. But that was a matter until now for the somebodies who were tortured and who displayed their scars at antifascist conferences. That suddenly you yourself are the Somebody, is grasped only with difficulty. That, too, is a kind of alienation.

If from the experience of torture any knowledge at all remains that goes beyond the plain nightmarish, it is that of a great amazement and a foreignness in the world that cannot be compensated by any sort of subsequent human communication. Amazed, the tortured person experienced that in this world there can be the other as absolute sovereign, and sovereignty revealed itself as the power to inflict suffering and to destroy. The dominion of the torturer over his victim has nothing in common with the power exercised on the basis of social contracts, as we know it. It is not the power of the traffic policeman over the pedestrian, of the tax official over the taxpayer, of the first lieutenant over the second lieutenant. It is also not the sacral sovereignty of past absolute chieftains or kings; for even if they stirred fear, they were also objects of trust at the same time. The king could be terrible in his wrath, but also kind in his mercy; his autocracy was an exercise of authority. But the power of the torturer, under which the tortured moans, is nothing other than the triumph of the survivor over the one who is plunged from the world into agony and death.

Astonishment at the existence of the other, as he boundlessly asserts himself through torture, and astonishment at what one can become oneself: flesh and death. The tortured person never ceases to be amazed that all those things one may, according to inclination, call his soul, or his mind, or his consciousness, or his identity, are destroyed when there is that cracking and splintering in the shoulder joints. That life is fragile is a truism he has always known—and that it can be ended, as Shakespeare says, "with a little pin." But only through torture did he learn that a living person can be transformed so thoroughly into flesh and by that, while still alive, be partly made into a prey of death.

Whoever has succumbed to torture can no longer feel at home in the world. The shame of destruction cannot be erased. Trust in the world, which already collapsed in part at the first blow, but in the end, under torture, fully, will not be regained. That one's fellow man was experienced as the antiman remains in the tortured person as accumulated horror. It blocks the view into a world in which the principle of hope rules. One who was martyred is a defenseless prisoner of fear. It is *fear* that henceforth reigns over him. Fear—and also what is called resentments. They remain, and have scarcely a chance to concentrate into a seething, purifying thirst for revenge.

How Much Home
Does a Person Need?

THE ROAD led through the wintry night in the Eifel, on smugglers' routes to Belgium, whose custom officials and policemen would have refused us a legal crossing of the border, for we were coming into the country as refugees, without passport and visa, without any valid national identity. It was a long way through the night. The snow lay knee-high; the black firs did not look any different from their sisters back home, but they were already Belgian firs; we knew that they did not want us. An old Jew in rubber overshoes, which he was constantly losing, clung to the belt of my coat, groaned and promised me all the riches of the world if only I allowed him to hold on to me now; his brother in Antwerp was an important and powerful man, he said. Somewhere, perhaps in the vicinity of the city Eupen, a truck picked us up and drove us deeper into the country. The next morning my young wife and I stood in the post office at the railway station of Antwerp and telegraphed in faulty school French that we had arrived safely. Heureusement arrivé—that was in the beginning of January 1939. Thereafter I crossed so many borders illegally that even now it still seems strange and wondrous to me when I pass a customs post in my car, well provided with all the necessary travel papers. In the process, my heart always beats rather heavily, obeying a Pavlovian reflex.

After we had arrived so "safely" in Antwerp and had confirmed this in a cable to the members of our family who had remained at home, we

41

exchanged the rest of our money, altogether fifteen marks and fifty pfennigs, if I recall correctly. That was the wealth with which we were to begin a new life, as it is said. The old one had forsaken us. For always? For always. But that I know only now, almost twenty-seven years later. With a few foreign bills and coins we entered exile. What misery. Whoever didn't know it was taught later by daily life in exile that the etymology of the German word for misery, whose early meaning implies exile, still contains its most accurate definition.

Anyone who is familiar with exile has gained many an insight into life but has discovered that it holds even more questions. Among the answers there is the realization, which at first seems trivial, that there is no return, because the re-entrance into a place is never also a recovery of the lost time. Among the questions, however, which on the very first day weigh the exile down, so to speak, and never leave him again, is one that I will attempt to illuminate in this essay—in vain, as I already know before I've really begun: how much home does a person need? What I can discover in this process will have little general validity, for I am posing the question from the very specific situation of someone who was exiled from the Third Reich—moreover, someone who, to be sure, left his country because under the given circumstances he would have wanted to leave it anyhow, but in addition went into exile because he *had* to. For many reasons then, my considerations will contrast very clearly with the ones of those Germans, for example, who were expelled from their homelands in the East. They lost their possessions, homestead, business, fortune, or perhaps only a modest job; beyond that, they lost the land, meadows and hills, a forest, a silhouette of a city, the church in which they had been confirmed. We lost all this too, but we also lost the people: the schoolmate from the same bench, the neighbor, the teacher. They had become informers or bullies, at best, embarrassed opportunists. And we lost our language. But of that, later.

Our exile was also not comparable to the self-exile of those emigrants who fled the Third Reich exclusively because of their ideology. For them it was possible to come to terms with the Reich, to return—be it remorsefully, be it only in silent loyalty—which some of them did, like the German novelist Ernst Glaeser. For us, who in those days were not allowed to return, and today therefore cannot return, the problem arises in a more urgent and compelling way. There is an anecdote about this, which will be cited here not because of its humorous value but only because of its usefulness as an illustration. The novelist Erich Maria Remarque, it is told, was repeatedly visited after 1933 at his home in Ticino by emissaries of Goebbel's ministry, because they wanted to induce the emigré writers who were "aryan" and thus never completely dominated by evil to return, to convert. When Remarque remained aloof, the envoy of the Reich finally asked him: For God's sake, man, aren't you homesick? Homesick, what do you mean? Remarque is said to have replied. Am I a Jew?

As far as I was concerned, I certainly was a Jew, as I had come to realize in 1935 after the proclamation of the Nuremberg Laws, and therefore I did suffer and still suffer from homesickness, a nasty, gnawing sickness, which does not have a folk song–like, homey quality, nor at all one sanctioned by emotional conventions, and of which one cannot speak in the Eichendorff tone.[7] I felt it piercingly for the first time when I stood at the exchange counter in Antwerp with fifteen marks, fifty, and it has left me as little as the memory of Auschwitz, or of torture, or of my return from the concentration camp, when once again I was back in the world, with a live weight of forty-five kilograms, wearing a striped prisoner's suit, and—after the death of the only person for whose sake I had held on to life for two years—doubly wanting.

What was, what is this homesickness of those who were expelled from the Third Reich both for their ideology and their pedigree? In this connection I reluctantly make use of a concept that only yesterday was the vogue, but there is probably not a more fitting one: my, our home-sickness was alienation from the self. Suddenly, the past was buried and one no longer knew who one was. At that time I still did not bear the French-sounding pen name with which I sign my works today. My identity was bound to a plain German name and to the dialect of my more immediate place of origin. But since the day when an official decree forbade me to wear the folk costume that I had worn almost exclusively from early childhood on, I no longer permitted myself the dialect. Then the name by which my friends had always called me, with a dialect coloring, no longer made much sense either. It was just about good enough for entry into the register of undesirable aliens at the city hall of Antwerp, where Flemish officials pronounced it in such a strange way that I scarcely understood it. And my friends, too, with whom I had spoken in my native dialect, were obliterated. Only they? Oh no; everything that had filled my consciousness—from the history of my country, which was no longer mine, to the landscape images, whose memory I suppressed—had become intolerable to me since that morning of the 12th of March 1938, on which the blood-red cloth with the black spider on a white field had waved even from the windows of out-of-the-way farmsteads. I was a person who could no longer say "we" and who therefore said "I" merely out of habit, but not with the feeling of full possession of my self. Sometimes it happened that in a conversation with my more or less benevolent Antwerp hosts I casually interjected: With us at home that is different. "Bij ons"; to the people with whom I was speaking that sounded like the most natural thing in the world. I, however, blushed, because I knew that it was a presumption. I was no longer an I and did not live within a We. I had no passport, and no past, and no money, and no history. There was only a line of ancestors, but it consisted of sad landless knights, stricken by an anathema. In addition, they had been subsequently deprived of their right of residence, and I had to take their ghosts along into exile.

"V'n wie kimmt Ihr?"—where do you come from, I was asked occasionally in Yiddish by a Polish Jew, for whom wandering and expulsion were just as much family history as for me a permanence of abode that had become meaningless. If I answered that I came from Hohenems, he naturally could not know where that is. And wasn't my origin, after all, completely unimportant? His ancestors had trudged with their bundle through the villages around Lvov, mine—in a caftan between Feldkirch and Bregenz. There was no longer any difference. The SA and SS men were not quite as good as the cossacks. And the man whom at home they called the Führer was much worse than the Czar. The itinerant Jew had more of a home than I.

If I am permitted already at this point to give a first and tentative answer to the question of how much home a person needs, I would say: all the more, the less of it he can carry with him. For there is, after all, something like a transportable home, or at least an ersatz for home. That can be religion, like the Jewish one. "Next year in Jerusalem," the Jews have promised themselves for generations during their Passover ritual, but it wasn't at all a matter of really getting to the Holy Land; rather it sufficed to pronounce the formula together and to know that one was united in the magic domain of the tribal God Yahweh.

Money can also be an ersatz for home. I still see before me the Jew from Antwerp, who in 1940, on his flight from the German conquerors, was sitting in a Flemish meadow, taking American bills from his shoe and counting them slowly and seriously. How fortunate you are to carry so much cash with you! another man said to him enviously. And in a dignified manner the counter of the bills answered him in his Flemish that was intermingled with Yiddish: "In dezen tijd behoord de mens bij zijn geld"—in these times a man belongs to his money. He carried his home with him in good American currency: *ubi Dollar ibi patria.*

Fame and esteem, too, can temporarily stand for home. In the memoirs of Heinrich Mann, *Ein Zeitalter wird besichtigt,* I read the following lines: "My name had been mentioned to the Mayor of Paris. He came towards me with extended arms: C'est vous, l'auteur de l'Ange Bleu! That is the highest peak of fame that I know." The great writer meant it ironically, for apparently he was offended that a French personage knew of him only that he had written a novel on which the film "The Blue Angel" was based. How thankless great writers can be! Heinrich Mann was safe and secure in the land of fame, even if this fame might have been only partly recognizable in a comic way in the legs of Marlene Dietrich.

As for me, lost in the line of refugees who queued up in front of the Antwerp Jewish Aid Committee for their weekly assistance, I was completely uprooted. The émigré writers of the German tongue, who at that time were famous or at least somewhat known and whose documentations of exile are now collected in the volume *Verbannung,* put out by Wegner Publishers, met in Paris, Amsterdam, Zurich, Sanary-sur-mer, New York. They too had worries and talked about visas, residence permits, and hotel bills. But their conversations also dealt with the review of a recently published book, a meeting of the Writers' Association, or an international antifascist congress. Furthermore, they lived in the illusion that they were the voice of the "true Germany," a voice that could be loudly raised abroad for the Fatherland enchained by National Socialism. Nothing like that for us anonymous ones. No game with the imaginary true Germany, which we had brought along with us, no formal ritual of a German culture preserved in exile for better days. The nameless refugees lived a social existence that was truer to German and international reality. This determined a consciousness that allowed, demanded, forced a more thorough recognition of reality. They knew that they were outcasts and not curators of an invisible museum of German intellectual history. They understood better that they had been made homeless, and since they did not possess any kind of mobile substitute for home, they could perceive more clearly how much a person needs a home.

Only reluctantly, of course, will I permit myself to be regarded as a straggler of the Blood and Soil army, and therefore I want to state clearly that I am also well aware of the enrichments and opportunities that homelessness offered us. I know how to appreciate the broader view of the world that emigration gave us. I went abroad and didn't know much more of Paul Eluard than his name, but I regarded a writer named Karl Heinrich Waggerl as an important literary figure. I have twenty-seven years of exile behind me, and my spiritual compatriots are Proust, Sartre, Beckett. Only I am still convinced that one must have compatriots in village and city streets if the spiritual ones are to be fully enjoyed, and that a cultural internationalism thrives well only in the soil of national security. Thomas Mann lived and discoursed in the Anglo-Saxon, international atmosphere of California, and with the strength of national self-assurance he wrote the exemplarily German *Doktor Faustus*. One has only to read Sartre's book *Les mots* and compare it with the autobiography *Le Traitre* of his pupil, the émigré André Gorz: in the case of Sartre, the full-blooded Frenchman, the surmounting and dialectic assimilation of the heritage of the Sartres and the Schweitzers, which give his internationalism worth and significance; in the case of Gorz, the half-Jewish Austrian émigré, a hectic search for identity, behind which there is nothing else but the longing for just that rootedness in a homeland from which Sartre freed himself in a proud and manly way. One must have a home in order not to need it, just as in thinking one must have mastery of the field of formal logic in order to proceed beyond it to more fertile regions of the mind.

But it is time to explain what I actually mean by this home that seems so essential to me. When we think about it, we must free ourselves of traditional, romantically stereotyped notions, which, to be sure, we will encounter again in a changed form, as transformed concepts, at a higher point on the spiral of thought. Reduced to the positive-psychological basic content of the idea, home is *security*. If I think back on the first days of exile in Antwerp, I still have the memory of a staggering on shaky ground. The mere fact that one could not decipher people's faces was frightening. I was having a beer with a big, coarse-boned, square-skulled man, who may have been a respectable Flemish citizen, perhaps even a patrician, but could just as well have been a suspicious harbor tough about to punch me in the face and lay hands on my wife. Faces, gestures, clothes, houses, words (even if I halfway understood them) were sensory reality, but not interpretable signs. There was no order for me in this world. Was the smile of the police official who checked our papers good-natured, indifferent, or mocking? Was his deep voice resentful or full of goodwill? I didn't know. Did the old bearded Jew, whose gurgling sounds I nevertheless grasped as sentences, mean it well with us or did he hate us, because by our mere presence on the streets of the city we incited against him the native population, which was already tired of foreigners, afflicted by economic troubles and therefore tending toward antisemitism? I staggered through a world whose signs remained as inscrutable to me as Etruscan script. Unlike the tourist, however, for whom such things may be a piquant form of alienation, I was dependent on this world full of riddles. The man with the square skull, the police agent with the resentful voice, the gurgling Jew were my lords and masters. At times I felt more vulnerable before them than before the SS man at home, because of him I had at least known with certainty that he was stupid and mean and that he was after my life.

Home is security, I say. At home we are in full command of the dialectics of knowledge and recognition, of trust and confidence. Since we know them, we recognize them and we trust ourselves to speak and to act —for we may have justified confidence in our knowledge and recognition. The entire field of the related words loyal, familiar, confidence, to trust, to entrust, trusting belongs in the broader psychological area of feeling secure. One feels secure, however, where no chance occurrence is to be expected, nothing completely strange to be feared. To live in one's homeland means that what is already known to us occurs before our eyes again and again, in slight variants. That can lead to desolation and to intellectual wilting in provincialism—if one knows only one's homeland and nothing else. If one has no home, however, one becomes subject to disorder, confusion, desultoriness.

At most, it can be objected that exile is perhaps not an incurable disease, since one can make a home of foreign countries by a long life in them and with them; that is called finding a new home. And it is correct inasmuch as slowly, slowly one learns to decipher the signs. Possibly, one can be so much "at home" in the foreign land that in the end one has the

ability to place people socially and intellectually on the basis of their
speech, their features, their clothes; that one recognizes at first glance the
age, the function, the financial value of a house; that one effortlessly links
one's new fellow citizens with their history and folklore. Nevertheless,
even in this favorable instance, for the exiled person who came to the
new country already as an adult, penetrating the signs will be not a spontaneous but rather an intellectual act, one combined with a certain expenditure of mental effort. Only those signals that we absorbed very early,
that we learned to interpret at the same time as we were gaining possession of our external world, become constitutional elements and constants
of our personality. Just as one learns one's mother tongue without knowing its grammar, one experiences one's native surroundings. Mother
tongue and native world grow with us, grow into us, and thus become
the familiarity that guarantees us security.

And here we encounter once again the traditional concept of home,
imparted to us by folk song and banal wisdom of proverbs, and which I
had temporarily avoided. What unwelcome reminiscences it wafts with it!
Fairy tales of an old nanny, mother's face above the bed, the fragrance of
lilacs from the neighbor's garden. And why not even spinning rooms and
rounds by the linden too, which people such as we know only from literature anyway? One would like to dispel the embarrassingly sweet tones that
are associated with the word home and that call forth a rather disturbing
series of concepts: regional arts and crafts, regional literature, regional
foolery of all kinds. But they are stubborn, keep close to our heels, demand
their effect. Heaven forbid, one need not immediately think of intellectual inferiority upon hearing the word homeland. Let Carossa be the
mediocre writer that he was. What, however, would Joyce be without
Dublin, Joseph Roth without Vienna, Proust without Illiers? The stories
of the housekeeper Françoise and Aunt Leonie in *Recherche* are also
regional literature. That reactionary indolence has taken over the entire
complex of ideas associated with home does not obligate us to ignore it.
Therefore, once again very clearly: there is no "new home." Home is the
land of one's childhood and youth. Whoever has lost it remains lost himself, even if he has learned not to stumble about in the foreign country as
if he were drunk, but rather to tread the ground with some fearlessness.

It is important to me here to determine the scope and effect of the
loss of home that befell us exiles from the Third Reich, and thus I must

explain in greater detail what until now I have mentioned only briefly. All the implications of this loss became truly clear to me only when, in 1940, my homeland followed after me in the form of the German conqueror troops. An especially frightening experience occurs to me, which I had in 1943, shortly before my arrest. In those days our resistance group had a base in a girl's apartment; the copying machine on which we produced our illegal fliers was kept there. On occasion the far too fearless young person, who later paid with her life, had casually mentioned in conversation that there were also German soldiers living in her house. In regard to the security of our quarters, however, this had appeared to us to be more favorable than not. Well, one day it happened that the German living below our hiding place felt disturbed in his afternoon rest by our talk and our doings. He climbed the stairs, pounded on the door, and stepped noisily across the threshold: an SS man with the black lapels and the woven insignia—of all things—of the Secret Service! Every one of us was pale with deadly fear, because in the next room stood the implements of our propaganda work, which oh so little endangered the existence of the Reich. The man, however, in his unbuttoned uniform jacket, with dishevelled hair, staring at us with sleep-drugged eyes, did not have any intentions appropriate to his trade as a hunting dog. Bellowing, he demanded only peace for himself and his comrade, who was tired from night duty. He made his demand—and for me this was the truly frightening part of the episode— in the dialect of my more immediate native region. I had not heard this accent for a long time, and for this reason there stirred within me the mad desire to answer him in his own dialect. I was in a paradoxical, almost perverse emotional state of trembling fear and, at the same time, surging intimate cordiality; for the fellow, who at this moment, to be sure, was not exactly after my life, but whose joyfully fulfilled task it was to take people like me in as large numbers as possible to a death camp, appeared to me suddenly as a potential friend. Was it not enough to address him in his, my language in order to then celebrate our regional patriotism and our reconciliation over a glass of wine?

Fortunately, fear and the control of reason were strong enough to hold me back from the absurd plan. I stammered French phrases of apology, which apparently calmed him. Slamming the door, the man left the place of subversion and me, the destined quarry of his soldier's duty that was enlivened by the passion of a hunter. At that moment I understood *completely* and forever that my home was enemy country and that the good comrade was sent here from the hostile homeland to wipe me out.

It was a rather banal experience. But nothing similar could ever have happened to a German refugee from the East, just as little as to an émigré from Hitler who was building castles of German culture in the air in New York or California. The German refugee from the East knows that a foreign power has taken his land from him. The cultural émigré, who was living in safety, believed that he was still spinning the thread of destiny of a German nation that was overwhelmed only temporarily and likewise by a foreign power, National Socialism. We, however, had not lost our country, but had to realize that it had never been ours. For us, whatever was linked with this land and its people was an existential mis- understanding. What we believed to have been our first love was, as they said there, racial disgrace. What we thought had constituted our nature —was it ever anything else but mimicry? Given some intellectual honesty, it was quite impossible for us, who during the war lived under the occupa- tion by the hostile homeland, to think of our country as oppressed by a foreign power: in too good a mood were our compatriots whom we, hid- den behind Belgian languages, disguised in clothes of Belgian cut and taste, happened to meet in the streets and taverns. If we entered into a conversation with them in deliberately broken German, they declared themselves all too unanimously for their Führer and his undertakings. With the strong voices of trusting youth they sang that they wanted to march against England. And often, while marching, they also struck up a rather stupid song that said that the Jews roamed back and forth and through the Red Sea until the waves engulfed them and the world had peace; that too was rhythmically powerful and rang of approval. In such form our homeland had caught up with us, and in such manner the bell peal of our native language resounded in our ears.

One will understand better now what I meant when I spoke of the nature of our homesickness, which was totally new and not determined by any conventional emotions recorded in literature. Traditional home- sickness—well, yes, we had that too, as a small extra. We drew it from within us with pretentious nostalgia (for we were not entitled to it) whenever we exiles spoke with the natives about our homeland. Then it was there and swelled in tearful bliss, for, whether we liked it or not,

toward the Belgians we had to act as though we were Germans or Aus-
trians; to be more exact: we really were that in these moments, since the
people with whom we were conversing forced our homeland upon us and
prescribed the role we were to play. Traditional homesickness was for us,
and is for everyone who takes pleasure in its bitter-sweetness, comforting
self-pity. But there was a constant undercurrent of awareness that we had
appropriated it illegally. There were times when, relaxed by alcohol, we
sang our Antwerp acquaintances native songs in our dialect, told them
about the mountains and rivers back home, and secretly wiped our eyes.
What emotional fraud! Journeys home with falsified papers and stolen
pedigree! We had to mime what we were, but hadn't the right to be.
What a foolish, sham undertaking!

Genuine homesickness, Thomas Mann's "Hauptwehe," if, with due
respect, I am permitted to steal from him, was of a different kind and
afflicted us when we were by ourselves. Then there were no more songs,
no effusive evocation of lost landscapes, no moist eye that at the same
time winked, asking for complicity. Genuine homesickness was not self-
pity, but rather self-destruction. It consisted in dismantling our past piece
by piece, which could not be done without self-contempt and hatred for
the lost self. The hostile home was destroyed by us, and at the same time
we obliterated the part of our life that was associated with it. The combination of hatred for our homeland and self-hatred hurt, and the pain
intensified most unbearably when, during the strenuous task of self-
destruction, now and then traditional homesickness also welled up and
claimed its place. What we urgently wished, and were socially bound, to
hate, suddenly stood before us and demanded our longing. A totally impossible, neurotic condition for which there is no psychoanalytic remedy.
The only therapy could have been history in practice. I mean the German
revolution and with it the homeland's strongly expressed desire for our
return. But the revolution did not take place, and our return was nothing
but an embarrassment for our homeland, when finally the National Socialist power was crushed from without.

In the years of exile our relationship to our homeland was akin to
that toward our mother tongue. In a very specific sense we have lost it too
and cannot initiate proceedings for restitution. In the aforementioned
book *Verbannung*, a collection of exile documents of German writers,
I read notes by the philosopher Günther Anders, in which he says: "No

one can move about for years exclusively irr languages that he has not mastered and at best parrots poorly, without falling victim to his inferior speech. . . . While we had not yet learned our English, French, or Spanish, our German began to crumble away piece by piece, and for the most part so imperceptibly and gradually that we did not notice the loss." This, however, by far does not encompass the entire language problem of the exiled. Instead of a "crumbling away" of the mother tongue, I would rather speak of its shrinking. We moved about not only in the foreign language, but also, when we did make use of German, in the narrowing confines of a vocabulary that constantly repeated itself. By necessity, conversations with our comrades in misfortune revolved about the same topics: at first about questions of livelihood, residence permits, and travel papers; later, under the German occupation, about the sheer danger of death. Those who spoke with us did not supply our language with any new substance; they only mirrored our own. Always, we turned in a circle of the same topics, same words, same phrases, and at best we enriched our speech in a most ugly way by carelessly introducing expressions from the language of our host country.

There, in the hostile homeland, the evolution of the language took its course. Not that it was a beautiful language that emerged there, not that. But it was—along with enemy bomber, enemy action, front control station, indeed even along with all the actual Nazi slang—a language of *reality*. All developed speech is figurative, whether it tells us of a tree that defiantly stretches a bare branch toward the sky, or of the Jew who infuses Near Eastern poison into the German national body. The material for metaphor is always provided by evident reality. We were shut out from German reality and therefore also from the German language. Most of the exiles denied themselves the bits of it that were drifting from Germany to the occupied countries anyway, with the theoretically valid, but in practice only partially useful, argument that there the German language was being corrupted and they had the mission to keep it "pure." At the same time they partly spoke their émigré "Chinese," partly an artificial language that was being marred before our eyes by wrinkles of old age. And in addition they did not suspect how much of the linguistic heritage or, if you will, linguistic rubbish from this time would survive long after Hitler's collapse and, for its part, was destined to pass into the literary language.

Others, like myself, made the hopeless attempt to cling to the advancing German language. Daily, in spite of extreme aversion, I read the "Brüsseler Zeitung," the organ of the German occupying power in the West. It did not ruin my language, but it also did not help it along. For I was excluded from the fate of the German community and thus from its language. "Enemy bomber," fine, but for me these were the German bombers that were laying the cities of England in ruins, and not the flying fortresses of the Americans, which were attending to the same business in Germany. The meaning of every German word changed for us, and finally, whether we resisted or not, our mother tongue became just as inimical as the one they spoke around us. Here, too, our fate was very different from that of those emigrants who lived in safety in the United States, in Switzerland, in Sweden. The words were laden with a given reality, which was the threat of death. "Again you fill copse and valley"—there was not a single word here that the murderer standing before us with drawn dagger could not also have used frequently.[8] Copse and valley, that is where one perhaps tried to hide. But one was tracked down in the misty sheen. And need I even say that the so oppressive reality content of our mother tongue, which stifled us in German-occupied exile, was of terrible permanence and still heavily burdens our language?

Not to the same degree, however, that our mother tongue proved to be hostile, did the foreign one become a real friend. It behaved and still behaves in a reserved manner and receives us only for brief formal visits. One calls on it, comme on visite des amis, which is not the same as dropping in on friends. La table will never be the table; at best one can eat one's fill at it. Even individual vowels, and though they had the same physical qualities as our native ones, were alien and have remained so. It occurs to me how in the first days of exile in Antwerp I heard a milkboy say "ja" at a house door while delivering his ware. He said it in Dutch with a Flemish accent and with exactly that dark A resembling an O that is usual in the same word in my native dialect. The "ja" was familiar and strange at the same time, and I understood that in the other language I would always be entitled only to temporary hospitality. The position of the boy's mouth when he said "ja" was foreign to me. The door before which he spoke the word looked different from a house door at home. The sky above the street was a Flemish sky. Every language is part of a total reality to which one must have a well-founded right of ownership if one is to enter the area of that language with a good conscience and confident step.

I have tried to examine and track down the meaning of the loss of home and mother tongue for us who were exiled from the Third Reich. The question, however, of what, apart from personal fate, home means in general for contemporary man thrusts itself upon one, and the title of my essay demands an answer. The temper of the epoch is not favorable to the idea of homeland, that is obvious. Whoever hears talk of it immediately thinks of narrow nationalism, of territorial claims by associations of expellees, of things in the past. Homeland—is that not a fading value, a concept dragged along from bygone days, still laden with emotion but already becoming meaningless and no longer having a tangible correspondent in modern industrial society? We shall see. But first, with all due brevity, the relationship between homeland and fatherland must be clarified, because a widespread attitude claims to accept the idea of homeland in its regional, folkloristic limits at least as something of picturesque value, while fatherland is extremely suspicious to it as a demagogic catchword and a characteristic of reactionary obstinacy. L'Europe des patries—that does not sound good, is only the obsession of an old general, whom the destiny of our time will soon quickly pass over.

I am not an old general. I do not dream of national grandeur, do not find in my family album any army officers and high-ranking civil servants. Also, I have a deep aversion to riflemen's gatherings, choral celebrations, and festivals of national costumes. I am, in general, precisely what in Germany not all too long ago would have been called an egghead, and I know that I am not free of destructive tendencies. But since I am a qualified homeless person I dare to stand up for the value that homeland signifies, and I also reject the sharp-witted differentiation between homeland and fatherland, and in the end believe that a person of my generation can get along only poorly without both, which are one and the same. Whoever has no fatherland—that is to say, no shelter in an autonomous social body representing an independent governmental entity—has, so I believe, no homeland either. "Kde domow muj"—"where is my fatherland?" sang the Czechs when, in the supranational Austro-Hungarian monarchy, they could not consider or feel their Czech land to be either a homeland or a fatherland, since it was not an independent state. They sang these verses because they wanted to attain a fatherland and thereby realize their homeland. Good, one can argue, but that was the reaction of a culturally and economically oppressed people, who were "colonized" by the ruling German group of Austria. Wherever nations with equal rights voluntarily form a larger polity, they can preserve their homeland through the conservation of a regional linguistic particularism, with no further need of a fatherland in governmental form. Their fatherland will be bigger: tomorrow a Little Europe, day after tomorrow a Greater Europe, and in a future that still is not foreseeable, but beyond question swiftly approaching, the world.

I submit my doubts. On the one hand, I believe to have experienced with sufficient clarity how home ceases to be home as soon as it is not at the same time also fatherland. When my country lost its national independence on March 12, 1938, and was annexed to the Pan-German Reich, it became totally alien to me. The uniforms of the policemen, the mailboxes on the houses, the emblems on the municipal offices, many signs in front of the stores displayed new faces, and even the menus in the restaurants showed other dishes, unknown to me. On the other hand, the greater fatherland loses its quality as fatherland if it grows all too far beyond an area that can still be experienced as home. Then it becomes an empire that fills its inhabitants with imperial consciousness and a heated great-power nationalism, like the Soviet Union and the United States. If tomorrow the Americans conquered the entire continent, together with the Latin American states, their imperial consciousness would remain as it already is today. Then they would move with their families from New York to La Paz, just as today they move from New England to Iowa or California, with the elated feeling that all this wide land belongs to them and is subject to the president in the White House. They would then derive no more from their fatherland and homeland than they do today when, thanks more to the standardized commodities of the giant industries than to language, they perceive their empire between Texas and New Jersey as an encompassing social entity. Where General Motors is, is their pseudofatherland and their pseudohomeland.

Naturally, one can say: so what. It is no great misfortune for a person to lose his homeland and his fatherland. On the contrary, he grows with the area that he matter-of-factly regards as his own. Is not the emerging Little Europe, which in the traditional sense is neither fatherland nor homeland, already today for the Germans, French, Italians, Belgians, the

Dutch, and the Luxemburgers an accrued property? With the same assurance, so they say, they move about in Karlsruhe and Naples, Brest and Rotterdam. They imagine themselves in the situation of the man who is rich and therefore also footloose and to whom the *world* belongs already. After all, jets take him faster from Paris to Tokyo, from New York to Toronto than a slow train took me scarcely four decades ago from Vienna to a village in Tyrol. Modern man exchanges his home for the world. What a brilliant transaction!

La belle affaire! But one doesn't exactly have to be a dull obscurant, fixed to the spot, in order to doubt this too. For many a person who trades what yesterday meant home for a second-rate cosmopolitanism gives up the sparrow in hand for the kolibri in the bush. Just because someone travels in a subcompact from Fürth to the Côte d'Azur and there, on the terrace of the café, orders deux martinis, he immediately thinks he is a cosmopolite of the second half of the century and that he has already pocketed the profits from the world-for-home exchange. Only when he becomes sick and the médecin prescribes him a local remedy does he get gloomy thoughts about French pharmacology and sigh for Bayer products and the Herr Doktor. Superficial knowledge of the world and languages, gained through tourism and business trips, is no compensation for home. The barter proves to be a dubious one.

But this is not to say that future generations will not be able to, will not have to, get along very well without a homeland. What the French sociologist Pierre Bertaux calls the mutation of the human being, the psychic assimilation of the technological-scientific revolution, is unavoidable. The new world will be much more thoroughly one than the daring dream of a Greater Europe pictures it today. The objects of daily use, which at present we still imbue with emotion, will be fully fungible. Already, American city planners are thinking of turning the house into a consumable commodity in the future. One hears that at intervals of twenty to twenty-five years entire sections of the city will be demolished and rebuilt, since house repairs will be as little worthwhile as certain auto repairs already are. But in such a world, how would one still be able to form the concept of home at all? The cities, highways, service stations, the furniture, the electric household appliances, the plates, and the spoons will be the same everywhere. It is conceivable that the language of the future world will also be the purely functional means of communication that for the natural scientist it already is today. The physicists communicate in the language of mathematics; for the cocktail party in the evening, Basic English suffices. The developing world of tomorrow will certainly expel the homeland and possibly the mother tongue and will let them exist peripherally as a subject of specialized historical research only.

However, we have not reached that point yet. Not by far. What we call home still gives access to a reality that for us consists of perception through the senses. Unlike the physicist, who recognizes reality not in the pendulum swing of a control device but rather in a mathematical formula, we are dependent on seeing, hearing, touching. Perhaps I am not speaking only for my already declining generation of those around fifty when I say that we are accustomed to living with things that tell us stories. We need a house of which we know who lived in it before us, a piece of furniture in whose small irregularities we recognize the craftsman who worked on it. We need a city whose features stir at least faint memories of the old copperplate engraving in the museum. Not only for the city planners of tomorrow but also for the inhabitants, who settle at topographical points but are subject to eviction anyway, the reality of a city will consist of the statistical tables that anticipate demographic development, and in the construction plans and blueprints of new streets. Into our consciousness, however, its total reality still penetrates through the eye—the old Gottfried Keller's dear little window—and is assimilated in a mental process that we call remembering.[9]

Remembering. That is the cue, and our reflections swing back on their own to their main topic: the loss of home by an expellee from the Third Reich. He has aged and, in a time span that now already runs into decades, has had to learn that it was not a wound that was inflicted upon him, one that will scar over with the ticking of time, but rather that he is suffering from an insidious disease that is growing worse with the years.

For aging makes us dependent to an increasing degree on the memory of the past. If I think back to the first years of exile, then I know, to be sure, that already at that time I felt homesick and a longing for the past, but I also remember that to a certain extent both were offset by hope. The young person grants himself that unlimited advance credit that the world around him usually allows him too. He is not only who he is, but also who he will be. There I was with fifteen marks, fifty; there I was getting lost in the line of relief recipients, crouching in the deportation train, spooning my soup from a can. Exactly how to define myself I did not know, since my past and my origin had been confiscated from me, since I did not live in a house but in a barracks number so-and-so, and since I also bore the middle name Israel, which had not been given to me by my parents but rather by a man named Globke. That was not good. But it was also not fatal. For even if I was not a decipherable past and present, at least I was a future: perhaps a man who will kill an SS General, perhaps a worker in New York, a settler in Australia, an author in Paris writing in French, the clochard on the Seine quay having a good time with his bottle of rotgut.

But the credit of the person who is aging depletes. His horizon presses in on him, his tomorrow and day-after-tomorrow have no vigor and no certainty. He is only who he is. The future is no longer around him and therefore also not within him. He cannot plead change. He shows the world a naked present. But he can exist nevertheless, if in this present there harmoniously rests a "once was." Ah, you know, says the aging person, whose present is without a future but contains a socially undenied past—ah, you know, here you see perhaps only the simple bookkeeper, the mediocre painter, the asthmatic who is arduously panting up the stairs. You see the one that I am, not the one that I was. But the one that I *was* is also still part of myself, and there I can assure you on my honor that my mathematics teacher placed great hopes in me, that my first exhibition received brilliant reviews, that I was a good skier. Do please include that in the picture you are forming of me. Grant me the dimension of my past, otherwise I would be quite incomplete. It is not true, or at least not entirely true, that a human being is only what he has realized. What Sartre once said is not quite correct: namely, that for a life coming to its end, the end is the truth of the beginning. Was my story a pitiful one? Perhaps. But it wasn't so in all its stages. My potentialities of once are just as much part of me as my later failure or inadequate success. I have withdrawn into the past, it is the old age pension from which I exist. I'm living in peace with it, thank you, I'm not doing badly. Such are approximately the words of someone who is entitled to his past.

The person who was expelled from the Third Reich will never be able to utter or think them. He looks back—since the future after all is something that is in store only for the younger ones and therefore befits only them—and he doesn't detect himself anywhere. He lies unrecognizable in the ruins of the years 1933 to 1945. And not just starting today. I still recall very well those intellectually simple Jews from the mercantile trade who at the beginning of exile, while they populated the waiting rooms of exotic consulates, pointed out their social positions in Germany, which had just been destroyed. The one had owned a large clothing store in Dortmund, the other a highly regarded china shop in Bonn, and still another had even been named councillor of commerce and member of the Commercial Court. They quickly stopped all their bragging and silently and humbly joined the others, who had never held a thousand-mark bill in their hands. Amazingly soon they understood that in 1933 their customers in Dortmund and Bonn had voided all their purchases. Their past as a social phenomenon had been retracted by society; thus it was impossible to still retain it as a subjective, psychological possession. And the older they grew, the harder their loss became, even if they had long since been doing lucrative business with clothing and dishes in New York or Tel Aviv—at which, incidentally, only a relatively small number of them succeeded.

For some, however, it was not a matter of commercial goods, but rather of airy spiritual possessions, and there the loss of that which had been turned into a total desolation of the world. Only those who were already old at the time of their expulsion did not clearly recognize this. In the Gurs camp in southern France, where I spent a few months in 1941, there was interred at the same time the almost seventy-year-old poet Alfred Mombert from Karlsruhe, who had been renowned in his day. He wrote to a friend: "Everything flows off me like a great rain . . . Everything had to remain behind, everything. Apartment, sealed up by the Gestapo. Permission to take along—just think—a hundred Reichsmarks. I with my 72-year-old sister, together with the entire Jewish population of Baden and the Palatinate, from infant to the oldest graybeard, within a few hours to the train station, then transported off via Marseille, Toulouse, to a big internment camp in the Lower Pyrenees. Has anything similar ever happened to a German poet?" The almost unbearable lines are cited here only for the sake of the first and last sentences; between the two there gapes a contradiction that contains all the problems of our exile and whose solution one truly could not have demanded of the old man, who died in Switzerland a year after writing the letter. Everything flowed off like a great rain, that is correct. The past of the neoromantic poet Alfred Mombert, author of the book *Der himmlische Zecher*, flowed from the world on the day when a seventy-year-old man by the name of Alfred Israel Mombert was deported from Karlsruhe and no hand was lifted to protect him. And still, after the irreversible had happened, he wrote of himself as a "German poet." In the barracks of Gurs, hungry, plagued by vermin, perhaps brutalized by an ignorant policeman of the Vichy government, he could not possibly have recognized that for which many of us needed years of concentrated thought and probing: that only someone who writes poetry not merely *in* German but also *for* Germans, upon their express wish, can be a German poet; that when everything flows off, the last traces of the past will also be swept along. The hand that was not raised in his protection cast the old man out. His readers of yesterday, who did not protest against his deportation, had undone his verses. When he wrote the tragic letter, Mombert was no longer a German poet any more than the commercial councillor was a commercial councillor when he fetched himself an old winter coat from the Aid Committee. In order to be one or the other we need the consent of society. But if society repudiates that we ever were that, then we have also never been it. Mombert was not a German poet in the barracks of Gurs. That is the way the hand that did not stir when he was taken away had wanted it. He died without a past—and we can only hope that, since he did not know it, he died in some peace.

That everything flowed off like a great rain was experienced more profoundly by those who survived the Third Reich and had the time to come to terms with themselves. At the latest, they understood it on the day when for the first time they felt themselves aging. One ages badly in exile. Because a human being needs a home. How much of one? That, of course, was not a genuine question, merely the wording of a title about whose success one can argue. How much home a person needs cannot be quantified. And still, precisely at this time, when home is losing some of its repute, one is greatly tempted to answer the purely rhetorical question and say: he needs much home, more, at any rate, than a world of people with a homeland, whose entire pride is their cosmopolitan vacation fun, can dream of. One must resist the inadmissible heightening of emotions, which would tear us from the sphere of reflection into sentimentalism. Nietzsche comes to mind, with his cawing crows flying toward the town with whirring wings, and the winter snow that threatens the solitary one. Woe to him who has no home, the poem says.[10] One does not wish to seem effusive and suppresses his lyrical reminiscences. What remains is the most matter-of-fact observation: it is not good to have no home.

Resentments

Sometimes it happens that in the summer I travel through a thriving land. It is hardly necessary to tell of the model cleanliness of its large cities, of its idyllic towns and villages, to point out the quality of the goods to be bought there, the unfailing perfection of its handicrafts, or the impressive combination of cosmopolitan modernity and wistful historical consciousness that is evidenced everywhere. All this has long since been legendary and is a delight to the world. One scarcely need dwell on it. Statistics show that the man on the street is faring as well as I have always wished that he and everyone everywhere could, and for years his situation has been considered exemplary. What remains to be said, perhaps, is that I do not find much to talk about with the people I meet there on highways, in trains, in hotel lobbies, and who always show extreme politeness —and for that reason I cannot judge how far and how deep their apparent urbanity goes.

Now and then I have something to do with intellectuals. One cannot wish them more refined, modest, and tolerant. Nor more modern; and it always seems unreal to me when I think how many of them, who belong to my generation, only yesterday swore by Blunck and Griese.[11] Because not a trace of it can be found in our conversations on Adorno or Saul Bellow or Nathalie Sarraute.

The land through which I occasionally travel offers the world an example not only of economic prosperity but also of democratic stability and political moderation. It has certain territorial claims to make and is struggling for the reunification with that part of its national body that was unnaturally separated from it and now suffers under foreign tyranny. But its behavior in these questions is commendably discreet; as has long since been proved, its happy people want no part of national demagogues and agitators.

I feel uncomfortable in this peaceful, lovely land, inhabited by hard-working, efficient, and modern people. The reader has already guessed why: I belong to that fortunately slowly disappearing species of those who by general agreement are called the victims of Nazism. The people of whom I am speaking and whom I am addressing here show muted understanding for my retrospective grudge. But I myself do not entirely understand this grudge, not yet; and that is why I would like to become clear about it in this essay. I would be thankful to the reader if he were willing to follow me, even if in the hour before us he more than once feels the wish to put down the book.

I speak as a victim and examine my resentments. That is no amusing enterprise, either for the reader or for me, and perhaps I would do well to excuse myself at the start for the lack of tact that will unfortunately be displayed. Tact is something good and important—plain, acquired tact in everyday behavior, as well as tact of mind and heart. But no matter how important it may be, it is not suited for the radical analysis that together we are striving for here, and so I will have to disregard it—at the risk of cutting a poor figure. It may be that many of us victims have lost the feeling for tact altogether. Emigration, Resistance, prison, torture, concentration camp—all that is no excuse for rejecting tact and is not intended to be one. But it is a sufficient causal explanation. Let us begin then: without tact, with just that much literary decorum as my effort to be honest and the theme itself force upon me.

My task would be easier if I wanted to shift the problem into the area of political polemics. Then I could cite the books of Kempner, Reitlinger, and Hannah Arendt and, without any further intellectual effort, come to a rather obvious conclusion. It would follow that resentments persist in the victims because on the West German public scene personalities who were allied with the torturers continue to play a role, because in spite of the extension of the Statute of Limitations for major war crimes the criminals have a good chance to attain a venerable old age and triumphantly to outlive us. Their activity during their days of glory guarantees it. But what would be gained by such a polemic? Practically nothing. The cause of justice has been pleaded in our name by honorable Germans, better, more vigorously than we ourselves could do it. But I am not at all concerned with a justice that in this particular historical instance could only be hypothetical anyway. What matters to me is the description of the subjective state of the victim. What I can contribute is the analysis of the resentments, gained from introspection. My personal task is to justify a psychic condition that has been condemned by moralists and psychologists alike. The former regard it as a taint, the latter as a kind of sickness. I must acknowledge it, bear the social taint, and first accept the sickness as an integrating part of my personality and then legitimize it. A less rewarding business of confession cannot be imagined, and in addition it will subject my readers to an unusual test of patience.

Resentments as the existential dominant of people like myself are the result of a long personal and historical development. They were by no means evident on the day when I left the last of my concentration camps, Bergen-Belsen, and returned home to Brussels, which was really not my home. We, the resurrected, all looked approximately the way the photos from those days in April and May 1945, now stored in archives, show us: skeletons that had been revived with Anglo-American canned corned beef, toothless ghosts with shaven heads, just about useful enough to give testimony quickly and then to clear out to where they really belonged. But we were "heroes," namely to the extent to which we could believe the banners that were stretched over our streets and which read: Gloire aux Prisonniers Politiques! Except that the banners quickly faded, and the pretty social workers and Red Cross nurses, who had turned up in the first days with American cigarettes, tired of their efforts. Still, for quite some time there lasted what was for me a totally unprecedented social and moral status, and it elated me to the extreme: being what I was—a surviving Resistance fighter, Jew, victim of persecution by a universally hated regime—there was mutual understanding between me and the rest of the world. Those who had tortured me and turned me into a bug, as dark powers had once done to the protagonist of Kafka's *The Metamorphosis*, were themselves an abomination to the victorious camp. Not only National Socialism, *Germany* was the object of a general feeling that before our eyes crystallized from hate into contempt. Never again would this land "endanger world peace," as they said in those days. Let it live, but no more than that. As the potato field of Europe, let it serve this continent with its diligence, but with nothing other than that. There was much talk about the collective guilt of the Germans. It would be an outright distortion of the truth if I did not confess here without any concealment that this was fine with me. It seemed to me as if I had experienced their atrocities as collective ones. I had been just as afraid of the simple private in his field-gray uniform as of the brown-clad Nazi official with his swastika armband. I also could not rid myself of the sight of the Germans on a small passenger platform where, from the cattle cars of our deportation train, the corpses had been unloaded and piled up; not on a single one of their stony faces was I able to detect an expression of abhorrence. Let collective crime and collective guilt balance each other and produce the equilibrium of world morality. *Vae victis castigatisque.*

There was no reason, hardly a real possibility, for resentments to form. Certainly, I wanted no part of any compassion with a people that for me was laden with collective guilt, and it was rather indifferently that I helped some Quakerly inspired persons to load a truck that was being used children's clothes to impoverished Germany. The Jews who in this hour were already trembling with the pathos of forgiveness and reconciliation, whether their name was Victor Gollancz or Martin Buber, were almost as distasteful to me as those so-called re-educators from America, England, or France, who could scarcely wait to rush to Germany, West or East, in order to play the *Praeceptores Germaniae.* For the first time in my life I was in tune with the public opinion that resounded around me. I felt just fine in the entirely unaccustomed role of conformist. For me the potato-field and war-ruins Germany was a lost area of the globe. I avoided speaking its, my language and chose a pseudonym with a Romance ring. Which way the international political winds were blowing, that, of course, I didn't know. For while I fancied myself as the conqueror of those who yesterday had tortured me, the real victors were all set to work out plans for the losers that had nothing, but absolutely nothing more to do with potato fields. At the very moment when I was imagining that through the fate I had suffered I had finally caught up with world

opinion, the latter was about to transcend itself. I thought that I was right
in the middle of contemporary reality and was already thrown back onto
an illusion.

I had my first doubts in 1948, while passing through Germany on a
train. I chanced upon a page from the American occupation forces newspaper and skimmed a letter to the editor, in which the anonymous writer
said to the GI's: "Just don't act so big around here. Germany will become great and powerful again. Hit the road, you crooks." The letter
writer, who was apparently inspired partly by Goebbels and partly by
Eichendorff, had as little idea at that time as I myself that this Germany
was, in fact, destined to celebrate a most grandiose resurrection of might,
not in opposition to the khaki-clad transatlantic soldiers but with them.
I was puzzled only that there actually was such a letter writer and because
I heard a German voice that sounded different from the way I believed it
was obliged to sound for a long time to come: remorseful. In the following
years there was less and less talk of remorse. First the pariah Germany was
accepted into the community of nations, after that it was courted, finally
it had to be dispassionately reckoned with in the power game.

Under these circumstances—circumstances of an unprecedented economic, industrial, and military rise—one cannot reasonably demand of
someone that he go on tearing his hair and beating his breast. The Germans saw themselves absolutely as victims, since, after all, they had been
compelled to survive not only the winter battles of Leningrad and Stalin-
grad, not only the bombardments of their cities, not only the judgment of
Nuremberg, but also the dismemberment of their country. Thus, as can
all too easily be understood, they were not inclined to do more than to
take the past of the Third Reich and, in their own way, to "overcome" it,
as one said back then. In those days, at the same time as the Germans
were conquering the world markets for their industrial products and were
busy at home—not without a certain equanimity—with overcoming, our
resentments increased; or perhaps I must restrain myself and say only
that *my* resentments increased.

I witnessed how Germany's politicians, only a few of whom, if I was
properly informed, had distinguished themselves in the resistance movement, speedily and enthusiastically sought to affiliate with Europe. Effortlessly, they joined the new Europe to the other one that between 1940
and 1944 Hitler had already successfully begun to reorder according to

his own plan. Suddenly there was good reason for resentments. It was not at all necessary that in German towns Jewish cemeteries and monuments for resistance fighters be desecrated. Conversations like the one I had in 1958 with a South German businessman over breakfast in the hotel were enough. Not without first politely inquiring whether I was an Israelite, the man tried to convince me that there was no longer any race hatred in his country. The German people bear no grudge against the Jewish people, he said. As proof he cited his government's magnanimous policy of reparations, which was, incidentally, well appreciated by the young state of Israel. In the presence of this man, whose mind was so at ease, I felt miserable: Shylock, demanding his pound of flesh. *Vae victoribus!* Those of us who had believed that the victory of 1945, even if only in small part, had been ours too, were forced to relinquish it. The Germans no longer had any hard feelings toward the resistance fighters and Jews. How could these still demand atonement? Jewish-born men of the same stamp as a Gabriel Marcel showed themselves most eager to reassure their German contemporaries and fellow human beings. Only totally obstinate, morally condemnable hate, already censured by history, they said, clings to a past that was clearly nothing other than an operational mishap of German history and in which the broad masses of the German people had no part.

But to my own distress, I belonged to that disapproving minority with its hard feelings. Stubbornly, I held against Germany its twelve years under Hitler. I bore this grudge into the industrial paradise of the new Europe and into the majestic halls of the West. I "stuck out," as I once had in the camp because of poor posture at roll call; I attracted the disapproving attention no less of my former fellows in battle and suffering, who were now gushing over about reconciliation, than of my enemies, who had just been converted to tolerance. I preserved my resentments. And since I neither can nor want to get rid of them, I must live with them and am obliged to clarify them for those against whom they are directed.

There seems to be general agreement that the final say on resentments is that of Friedrich Nietzsche, in whose *Genealogy of Morals* we read: "... resentment defines such creatures who are denied genuine reaction, that of the deed, and who compensate for it through an imaginary revenge. ... The resentful person is neither sincere, nor naïve, nor honest and forthright with himself. His soul squints; his mind loves hiding places and back doors; everything concealed gives him the feeling that it is his world, his security, his balm. ..." Thus spake the man who dreamed of the synthesis of the brute with the superman. He must be answered by those who witnessed the union of the brute with the sub-human; they were present as victims when a certain humankind joyously celebrated a festival of cruelty, as Nietzsche himself has expressed it—in anticipation of a few modern anthropological theories.

But am I attempting this rejoinder in full command of my mental powers? Mistrustingly, I examine myself. It could be that I am sick, for after observing us victims, objective scientific method, in its lovely detachment, has already come up with the concept of the "concentration camp syndrome." I read in a recently published book about "Delayed Psychic Effects After Political Persecution" that all of us are not only physically but also mentally damaged. The character traits that make up our personality are distorted. Nervous restlessness, hostile withdrawal into one's own self are the typical signs of our sickness. It is said that we are "warped." That causes me to recall fleetingly the way my arms were twisted high behind my back when they tortured me. But it also sets me the task of defining anew our warped state, namely as a form of the human condition that morally as well as historically is of a higher order than that of healthy straightness. Thus I must delimit our resentments on two sides and shield them against two explications: that of Nietzsche, who morally condemned resentment, and that of modern psychology, which is able to picture it only as a disturbing conflict.

Vigilance is imperative. Seductive, consoling self-pity could entice. But one can believe me when I say that for me this is no problem. In the jails and camps of the Third Reich all of us scorned rather than pitied ourselves because of our helplessness and all-encompassing weakness. The temptation to reject ourselves has survived within us, as well as the immunity to self-pity. We don't believe in tears.

In pondering this question, it did not escape me that resentment is not only an unnatural but also a logically inconsistent condition. It nails every one of us onto the cross of his ruined past. Absurdly, it demands that the irreversible be turned around, that the event be undone. Resentment blocks the exit to the genuine human dimension, the future. I know that the time-sense of the person trapped in resentment is twisted around, dis-ordered, if you wish, for it desires two impossible things: regression into the past and nullification of what happened. But more on this later.

In any event, for this reason the man of resentment cannot join in the unisonous peace chorus all around him, which cheerfully proposes: not backward let us look but forward, to a better, common future!

To the very same degree that for me a fresh, calm look toward the future is too difficult, my persecutors of yesterday manage to find it too easy. Lame-winged as I am after exile, life in hiding, and torture, I can't keep up with the lofty ethical flights that a man like the French publicist André Neher propounds to us victims. We victims of persecution, the high-soaring man says, ought to internalize our past suffering and bear it in emotional asceticism, as our torturers should do with their guilt. But I must confess: I lack the desire, the talent, and the conviction for something like that. It is impossible for me to accept a parallelism that would have my path run beside that of the fellows who flogged me with a horsewhip. I do not want to become the accomplice of my torturers; rather, I demand that the latter negate themselves and in the negation coordinate with me. The piles of corpses that lie between them and me cannot be removed in the process of internalization, so it seems to me, but, on the contrary, through actualization, or, more strongly stated, by actively settling the unresolved conflict in the field of historical practice.

It has reached the point where one must defend oneself for thinking this way. I know, somebody will object that what I am presenting is a barbaric, primitive lust for revenge, which I have merely disguised in nice, or not-so-nice, at any rate, in highbrow terms, but which has fortunately been overcome by progressive morality. Self-confessed man of resentments that I am, I supposedly live in the bloody illusion that I can be compensated for my suffering through the freedom granted me by society to inflict injury in return. The horsewhip lacerated me; for that reason, even if I do not dare demand that the now defenseless thug be surrendered up to my own whip-swinging hand, I want at least the vile satisfaction of knowing that my enemy is behind bars. Thereupon I would fancy that the contradiction of my madly twisted time-sense were resolved.

It is not easy to reject the reproach that so simplifies the problem, and it is entirely impossible for me to refute the suspicion that I am drowning the ugly reality of a malicious instinct in the verbal torrent of an unverifiable thesis. I will have to take the risk. When I stand by my resentments, when I admit that in deliberating our problem I am "biased,"

I still know that I am the captive of the *moral truth* of the conflict. It seems logically senseless to me to demand objectivity in the controversy with my torturers, with those who helped them, and with the others, who merely stood by silently. The atrocity as atrocity has no objective character. Mass murder, torture, injury of every kind are objectively nothing but chains of physical events, describable in the formalized language of the natural sciences. They are facts within a physical system, not deeds within a moral system. The crimes of National Socialism had no moral quality for the doer, who always trusted in the norm system of his Führer and his Reich. The monster, who is not chained by his conscience to his deed, sees it from his viewpoint only as an objectification of his will, not as a moral event. The Flemish SS-man Wajs, who—inspired by his German masters—beat me on the head with a shovel handle whenever I didn't work fast enough, felt the tool to be an extension of his hand and the blows to be emanations of his psycho-physical dynamics. Only I possessed, and still possess, the moral truth of the blows that even today roar in my skull, and for that reason I am more entitled to judge, not only more than the culprit but also more than society—which thinks only about its continued existence. The social body is occupied merely with safeguarding itself and could not care less about a life that has been damaged. At the very best, it looks forward, so that such things don't happen again. But my resentments are there in order that the crime become a moral reality for the criminal, in order that he be swept into the truth of his atrocity.

SS-man Wajs from Antwerp, a repeated murderer and an especially adroit torturer, paid with his life. What more can my foul thirst for revenge demand? But if I have searched my mind properly, it is not a matter of revenge, nor one of atonement. The experience of persecution was, at the very bottom, that of an extreme *loneliness*. At stake for me is the release from the abandonment that has persisted from that time until today. When SS-man Wajs stood before the firing squad, he experienced the moral truth of his crimes. At that moment, he was with *me*—and I was no longer alone with the shovel handle. I would like to believe that at the instant of his execution he wanted exactly as much as I to turn back time, to undo what had been done. When they led him to the place of execution, the antiman had once again become a fellow man. If everything had taken place only between SS-man Wajs and me, and if an entire inverted pyramid of SS men, SS helpers, officials, Kapos, and medal-bedecked generals had not weighed on me, I would have died calmly and appeased along with my fellow man with the Death's Head insignia. At least that is the way it seems to me now.

But Wajs from Antwerp was only one of a multitude. The inverted pyramid is still driving me with its point into the ground. Thus the special kind of resentments, of which neither Nietzsche nor Max Scheler (who wrote on the subject in 1912) was able to have any notion. Thus also my scant inclination to be conciliatory—more precisely, my conviction that loudly proclaimed readiness for reconciliation by Nazi victims can only be either insanity and indifference to life or the masochistic conversion of a suppressed *genuine* demand for revenge. Whoever submerges his individuality in society and is able to comprehend himself only as a function of the social, that is, the insensitive and indifferent person, really does forgive. He calmly allows what happened to remain what it was. As the popular saying goes, he lets time heal his wounds. His time-sense is not dis-ordered, that is to say, it has not moved out of the biological and social sphere into the moral sphere. As a deindividualized, interchangeable part of the social mechanism he lives with it consentingly, and when he forgives, his behavior is analogous to the social reaction to crime, as the French trial lawyer Maurice Garçon described it in connection with the debate on the Statute of Limitations. "Already the child," so the *maître* instructs us, "who is reproached for a past lack of obedience, answers: but that's already past. This already-being-long-past appears to the child in the most natural way as an excuse. And we, too, regard the remoteness through time as the principle of the Statute of Limitations. A crime causes disquiet in society; but as soon as public consciousness loses the memory of the crime, the disquiet also disappears. The punishment that is temporally far removed from the crime, becomes senseless." This is correct to the point of being a platitudinous revelation—to the extent that we are dealing with society, or with the individual who incorporates himself morally into society and dissolves in its consensus. It has no relevance whatsoever for the person who perceives himself to be morally unique.

And thus, with the help of a trick, I have placed my mean irreconcilability in the shining light of morals and morality. Without a doubt, I will be reproached for this, and I must reply, since I am aware from the start that the overwhelming majority of the world's nonvictims will hardly

accept my justification. But it doesn't matter. In two decades of contemplating what happened to me, I believe to have recognized that a for-
giving and forgetting induced by social pressure is immoral. Whoever
lazily and cheaply forgives, subjugates himself to the social and biological
time-sense, which is also called the "natural" one. Natural consciousness
of time actually is rooted in the physiological process of wound-healing
and became part of the social conception of reality. But precisely for this
reason it is not only extramoral, but also *anti*moral in character. Man has
the right and the privilege to declare himself to be in disagreement with
every natural occurrence, including the biological healing that time brings
about. What happened, happened. This sentence is just as true as it is
hostile to morals and intellect. The moral power to resist contains the
protest, the revolt against reality, which is rational only as long as it is
moral. The moral person demands annulment of time—in the particular
case under question, by nailing the criminal to his deed. Thereby, and
through a moral turning-back of the clock, the latter can join his victim
as a fellow human being.

I cannot flatter myself that with these arguments I have convinced
anyone who is a member of the same nation as the criminals or who
merely as a nonvictim belongs to the greater community of all the uninjured in this world. But I am not at all speaking with the intention to
convince; I just blindly throw my word onto the scale, whatever it may
weigh. What will its weight be? That will depend in some measure on
whether I am able to check my resentments—which must necessarily form
part of their analysis—at least to the extent that they do not overrun their
subject. If I seek to delimit the area in which they are active, I must return
once again to what I have suggestively called collective guilt. The word is
forbidden, not just as of today, but already since 1946. For if the Germans
were to play the European role intended for them, one could not offend
them. There was hushing up, shame for having ever even coined such a
seemingly ill-considered term. Although I do not find it easy, I must stick
to it. But first I must adequately define it, whatever the risk.

Collective guilt. That is naturally sheer nonsense if it implies that the
community of Germans possessed a common consciousness, a common
will, a common initiative to act, and therein became culpable. But it is a
useful hypothesis if nothing else is meant by it than the objectively manifested *sum* of individual guilty conduct. Then there grows out of the guilt

of individual Germans—guilt of deed, guilt of omission, guilt of utterance, guilt of silence—the total guilt of a people. Before the concept of collective guilt can be applied, it must be freed of myth and mystification. Then it will lose its dark, ominous tone and be useful in the only way that it can: as a vague statistical statement.

Vaguely statistical, I say; for precise figures are lacking, and no one can determine how many Germans recognized, approved, or themselves committed the crimes of National Socialism, or in helpless revulsion allowed them to pass in their name. But every one of us victims had his own statistical experience, even if it was only approximate and cannot be expressed in numbers. After all, during the decisive years, we lived in the midst of the German people, whether in hiding under German occupation abroad, or in Germany itself, working in factories or imprisoned in jails and camps. For that reason, I could and can say that the crimes of the regime entered my consciousness as collective deeds of the people. There were those who, in the Third Reich, broke out of the Third Reich, even if only silently, through an angry glance at the SS Roll Call Officer Rakas, or through a compassionate smile for us, or by lowering their eyes in shame; but they were not numerous enough in my numberless statistics to tip the balance in their favor.

I have forgotten nothing, including the few brave people I encountered. They are with me: the disabled soldier Herbert Karp from Danzig, who in Auschwitz-Monowitz shared his last cigarette with me; Willy Schneider, Catholic worker from Essen, who addressed me by my already forgotten first name and gave me bread; the chemicals foreman, Matthäus, who said to me with an anguished sigh on June 6, 1944: "Finally, they have landed! But will the two of us hold out until they have won once for all?" I have many a good comrade. There was the *Wehrmacht* soldier from Munich, who tossed a burning cigarette through the cell bars after I had been tortured in Breendonk. There was the chivalrous Baltic engineer and the technician from Graz, whom I no longer recall by name and who saved me from perishing in a cable detachment in Buchenwald Dora. Sometimes I worry about their fate, which perhaps, which most likely, was not a good one.

My good comrades are not to be blamed, nor am I, that their weight is too slight as soon as they stand before me no longer in their singularity but in the midst of their people. A German poet wrote in a piece that is titled *"altbraun"* and that tries to describe the nightmare of the brown majority:

> ...and if some both in relation to many and to all are in the minority then they are much more so in relation to all than in relation to many and all form a stronger majority in relation to some than in relation to many ...

I had to do only with some, and in relation to them the many, who to me really had to appear as all, form an overwhelming majority. The upright men, whom I would gladly have saved, have already gone under in the mass of the indifferent, the malicious and vile, the shrews, the old fat ones and the young pretty ones, those intoxicated by their authority, who thought that it was a crime not only against the state but also against their own ego if they spoke with people like us in any other but a crude, domineering tone. The far-too-many were not SS men, but rather laborers, file clerks, technicians, typists—and only a minority among them wore the party badge. All in all, for me they were the German people. What was taking place around them and with us, they knew exactly. For they perceived the burnt smell from the nearby extermination camp as we did, and some wore clothes that only the day before had been taken on the selection ramps from the arriving victims. A hardy worker, the assembly foreman Pfeiffer, once proudly presented himself to me in a winter coat, a "Jew coat," as he said, that his skill had enabled him to procure. They found that everything was just right, and I am dead certain that they would have voted for Hitler and his accomplices if at that time, 1943, they had stepped up to the ballot box. Workers, petty bourgeois, academics, Bavarians, Saarlanders, Saxons: there was no difference. Whether the victim wanted to or not, he had to believe that Hitler really was the German people. My Willy Schneider and Herbert Karp and Foreman Matthäus did not stand a chance of prevailing against the mass of the people.

But it looks to me as if now I have "quantified," which is an inexpiable sin against the intellect, if one wants to believe the moral philosophers. It is not a matter of quantities, they say, but of qualitatively determined symbols and symbolic acts, of signs. Quelle vieille chanson! —and despite its age it has not become venerable. If anyone hopes to obstruct me with the reproach of inadmissible quantification, I ask him whether we do anything other than quantify in daily life, in legal life, in political, in economic, as well as in the higher and highest intellectual life. Whoever owns a hundred marks is no millionaire. Whoever scratches his opponent's skin in a brawl has not dealt him a serious injury. "Du bist Orplid, mein Land," has, so the reader's feeling tells him, less value than *War and Peace*.[12] The democratic statesman does not deal any differently with quantity than does the surgeon who must judge a malignant tumor or the musician who sets about conceiving an orchestral work. I, too, had to determine the quantity of good comrades on the one hand and of the scoundrels and indifferent ones on the other when, in the midst of the German people, I had to reckon every moment with falling victim to ritual mass murder. Whether I wanted to or not, I had to accept the notion of statistical collective guilt, and I am burdened with this knowledge in a world and a time that has proclaimed the collective innocence of the Germans.

I am burdened with collective guilt, I say; not they. The world, which forgives and forgets, has sentenced me, not those who murdered or allowed the murder to occur. I and others like me are the Shylocks, not only morally condemnable in the eyes of the nations, but already cheated of the pound of flesh too. Time did its work, very quietly. The generation of the destroyers—the gas chamber constructors, those ready at any time to sign their name to anything, the generals duty-bound to their Führer—is growing old with honor. To accuse the young would be just too inhuman, and according to universal concepts also unhistorical. After all, what does a twenty-one-year-old student who has grown up in the calm climate of a new German democracy have to do with the deeds of his fathers and grandfathers? Only stagnant, Old Testament, barbaric hate could come dragging its burden and want to load it onto the shoulders of innocent German youth. Accordingly, segments of the young people, fortunately not all, do protest with the sound consciousness of justice possessed by those who stand on the solid ground of their natural time-sense. In a German weekly I read the letter of an obviously young man from Kassel, who eloquently expresses the displeasure of the new German generations at the haters and the resentful, who—since they are in every respect out-of-date—are also bad. He writes: ". . . we are finally sick and tired of hearing again and again that our fathers killed six million Jews. How many innocent women and children did the Americans murder with their bombings, how many Boers did the British murder in the Boer War?" This protest confronts us with a moral vigor that is sure of its cause. One scarcely dares to object that the equation "Auschwitz = Boer internment camp" is faulty moral mathematics. For the entire world really does understand the young Germans' indignation at the resentful prophets of hate, and firmly sides with those to whom the future belongs. Future is obviously a value concept. What will be tomorrow is more valuable than what was yesterday. That is how the natural feeling for time will have it.

When I ask myself whether I hold against German youth what the older generation inflicted on me, I don't find the answer quite so easily. It is understandable that the young people are free of individual guilt and of the collective guilt that results from its summation. I must, and want to, grant them the advance in confidence that is due the future-oriented person. But possibly one can expect of these young people that they do not lay claim to their innocence as vigorously and impudently as the letter writer quoted above. For as long as the German nation, including its young and youngest age groups, does not decide to live entirely without history—and there is no sign that the world's most history-conscious national community suddenly would assume such a position—then it must continue to bear the responsibility for those twelve years that it certainly did not terminate itself. German youth cannot cite Goethe, Mörike, and Baron von Stein, and ignore Blunck, Wilhelm Schäfer, and Heinrich Himmler.[13] It will not do to claim national tradition for oneself where it was honorable and to deny it where, as dishonor incarnate, it cast a probably imaginary and certainly defenseless opponent from the community of man. If being German means being a descendent of Matthias Claudius, then surely it must also mean that one has the Nazi party poet Hermann Claudius in one's pedigree.[14] Thomas Mann knew that when he wrote in his essay "Germany and the Germans": "It is impossible for a thinking German to declare: I am the good, just, noble Germany in a white robe. ... Nothing that I have said to you about Germany came from foreign, cool, detached knowledge; I also have it within me, I have experienced it all myself."

The edition of the volume of essays from which I am quoting is called *Schulausgabe moderner Autoren*. I don't know whether Thomas Mann's essays actually are read in German schools and how they are commented on by the teachers. I can only hope that young Germans do not find the intellectual link-up with Thomas Mann overly difficult, and that the majority of young people do not share the indignation of the above-cited correspondent. To repeat: Hitler and his deeds will also continue to be a part of German history and German tradition.

And I enter into the realm of German history and historicity as I speak further of the victim's resentments. I am obliged, however, to define their objective task. Perhaps it is only concern for my own purification, but I hope that my resentment—which is my personal protest against the antimoral natural process of healing that time brings about, and by which I make the genuinely humane and absurd demand that time be turned back—will also perform a historical function. Were it to fulfill the task that I set it, it could historically represent, as a stage of the world's moral dynamics of progress, the German revolution that did not take place. This demand is no less absurd and no less moral than the individual demand that irreversible processes be reversible.

In order to clarify and simplify what I mean, I need only return to the conviction already expressed that the unresolved conflict between victims and slaughterers must be externalized and actualized, if both the overpowered and those who overpowered them are to succeed in mastering the past, a past that, despite its extreme oppositeness, they still have in common. Externalization and actualization: most certainly, they cannot consist in a revenge dealt out in proportion to what was suffered. I cannot prove it, but I am certain that there is no victim who would even have considered hanging the man Bogner, of the Auschwitz trial, in the Bogner swing. Even less would any sane person among us ever venture the morally impossible thought that four to six million Germans should be forcibly taken away to their death. Nowhere else could the *jus talionis* make less historic and moral sense than in this instance. It can be a matter neither of revenge on the one side nor of a problematic atonement, which has only theological meaning and therefore is not relevant for me, on the other. Of course, it cannot be a matter of settlement by force, which is historically unthinkable anyhow. What then is it a matter of—since I have spoken expressly of a settlement in the field of historical practice?

Well then, the problem could be settled by permitting resentment to remain alive in the one camp and, aroused by it, self-mistrust in the other. Goaded solely by the spurs of our resentment—and not in the least by a conciliatoriness that, subjectively, is almost always dubious and, objectively, hostile to history—the German people would remain sensitive to the fact that they cannot allow a piece of their national history to be neutralized by time, but must integrate it. If I remember rightly, it was Hans Magnus Enzensberger who once wrote that Auschwitz is Germany's past, present, and future. But unfortunately he is not what counts, for he and his moral peers are not the people. But if, in the midst of the world's silence, our resentment holds its finger raised, then Germany, as a whole and also in its future generations, would retain the knowledge that it was not Germans who did away with the dominion of baseness. It would then, as I sometimes hope, learn to comprehend its past acquiescence in the Third Reich as the total negation not only of the world that it plagued with war and death but also of its own better origins; it would no longer repress or hush up the twelve years that for us others really were a thousand, but claim them as its realized negation of the world and its self, as its own negative possession. On the field of history there would occur what I hypothetically described earlier for the limited, individual circle: two groups of people, the overpowered and those who overpowered them, would be joined in the desire that time be turned back and, with it, that history become moral. If this demand were raised by the German people, who as a matter of fact have been victorious and already rehabilitated by time, it would have tremendous weight, enough so that by this alone it would already be fulfilled. The German revolution would be made good, Hitler disowned. And in the end Germans would really achieve what the people once did not have the might or the will to do, and what later, in the political power game, no longer appeared to be a vital necessity: the eradication of the ignominy.

How this shall come about in actual practice, every German may picture for himself. This writer is not a German and it is not for him to give advice to this people. At best, he is able to imagine vaguely a national community that would reject everything, but absolutely everything, that it accomplished in the days of its own deepest degradation, and what here and there may appear to be as harmless as the Autobahns. Remaining within his exclusively literary frame of reference, Thomas Mann once expressed this in a letter: "It may be superstition," he wrote to Walter von Molo, "but in my eyes the books that could be printed in Germany between 1933 and 1945 are less than worthless and one ought not to touch them. An odor of blood and disgrace clings to them; they should all be reduced to pulp." The spiritual reduction to pulp by the German people, not only of the books, but of everything that was carried out in those twelve years, would be the negation of the negation: a highly positive, a redeeming act. Only through it would our resentment be subjectively pacified and have become objectively unnecessary.

But what an extravagant moral daydream I have abandoned myself to! Already I saw the faces of the German passengers on the station platform of 1945 grow pale at the sight of the piled corpses of my comrades and turn threateningly toward our, and their, tormentors. Thanks to my resentments and the German inner cleansing brought about by its traces, I already saw time turned backward. Did not a German tear from SS-man Wajs the shovel he used as a tool for beating? Did not a German woman receive the man who was dazed and battered after being tortured and nurse his wounds? What didn't I see in the unbridled past, which in the future was transformed and from then on was overcome, truly and forever!

Nothing of the sort will happen, I know, despite all the worthy efforts of German intellectuals, who to be sure really may be what others reproach them for: rootless. All recognizable signs suggest that natural time will reject the moral demands of our resentment and finally extinguish them. The great revolution? Germany will not make it good, and our rancor will have been for nothing. Hitler's Reich will, for the time being, continue to be regarded as an operational accident of history. Finally, however, it will be purely and simply history, no better and no worse than dramatic historical epochs just happen to be, bloodstained perhaps, but after all a Reich that also had its everyday family life. The picture of great-grandfather in his SS uniform will hang in the parlor, and the children in the schools will learn less about the selection ramps than about an astounding triumph over general unemployment. Hitler, Himmler, Heydrich, Kaltenbrunner—these will be names like Napoleon, Fouché, Robespierre, and Saint Just. Already today, after all, I read in a book that is titled *Über Deutschland* and contains imaginary dialogues between a German father and his very young son, that in the son's eyes there is no difference between Bolshevism and Nazism. What happened in Germany between 1933 and 1945, so they will teach and say, could have occurred anywhere else under similar circumstances, and no one will insist any further on the trifle that it did happen precisely in Germany and not somewhere else. In his book *Rückkehr zum Mauerwald* the former German general staff officer Prince Ferdinand von der Leyen writes: "... from one of our detachments came even more horrible news. SS units had broken into the houses there and from the upper floors they had thrown children, who were still unable to walk, through the windows onto the pavement." But such murder of millions as this, carried out by a highly civilized people, with organizational dependability and almost scientific precision, will be lumped with the bloody expulsion of the Armenians by the Turks or with the shameful acts of violence by the colonial French: as regrettable, but in no way unique. Everything will be submerged in a general "Century of Barbarism." We, the victims, will appear as the truly incorrigible, irreconcilable ones, as the antihistorical reactionaries in the exact sense of the word, and in the end it will seem like a technical mishap that some of us still survived.

I travel through the thriving land, and I feel less and less comfortable as I do. I cannot say that I am not received everywhere in a friendly and understanding manner. What more can people like me ask than that German newspapers and radio stations grant us the possibility to address grossly tactless remarks to German men and women, and on top of this to be remunerated for it? I know: even the most benevolent will finally have to become as impatient with us as that young correspondent cited earlier, who is "sick and tired of it." There I am with my resentments, in Frankfurt, Stuttgart, Cologne, and Munich. If you wish, I bear my grudge for reasons of personal salvation. Certainly. On the other hand, however, it is also for the good of the German people. But no one wants to relieve me of it, except the organs of public opinion-making, which buy it. What dehumanized me has become a commodity, which I offer for sale.

Fateful land, where some stand eternally in the light and the others eternally in the darkness. I travelled the length and breadth of it in the evacuation trains that, under the pressure of the final Soviet offensive, carried us from Auschwitz westward and later from Buchenwald north to Bergen-Belsen. When the tracks led us through the snow across a corner of Bohemian countryside, the peasant women came running to the death train with bread and apples and had to be chased off through shots into the air by the escort party. But in the Reich: faces of stone. A proud people. A proud people still. The pride has grown a bit stout, I'll admit. It no longer squeezes out between grinding jaws but gleams in the contentment of good conscience and the understandable joy of having made it once again. It no longer cites its heroism on the battlefield but the productivity that has no like in the entire world. Still, it is the old pride, and on our side it is the old helplessness. Woe to the conquered.

I must encapsulate my resentments. I can still believe in their moral value and their historical validity. Still, but how much longer? The very fact that I must ask myself such a question demonstrates the immensity and monstrosity of the natural time-sense. Perhaps already tomorrow it will lead me to self-condemnation, by having me see the moral desire for reversal as the half-brained chatter that it already is today for the rationally thinking know-it-alls. That will be the final victory for the proud people in which my Herbert Karp, Willy Schneider, Foreman Matthäus, and the few intellectuals of today are drowning. The fears of Nietzsche and Scheler actually were not warranted. Our slave morality will not triumph. Our resentments—emotional source of every genuine morality, which was always a morality for the losers—have little or no chance at all to make the evil work of the overwhelmers bitter for them. We victims must finish with our retroactive rancor, in the sense that the KZ argot once gave to the word "finish"; it meant as much as "to kill." Soon we must and will be finished. Until that time has come, we request of those whose peace is disturbed by our grudge that they be patient.

On the Necessity
and Impossibility
of Being a Jew

NOT SELDOM, when in conversation my partner draws me into a plural—that is, as soon as he includes my person in whatever connection and says to me: "We Jews . . ."—I feel a not exactly tormenting, but nonetheless deep-seated discomfort. I have long tried to get to the bottom of this disconcerting psychic state, and it has not been very easy for me. Can it be, is it thinkable that I, the former Auschwitz inmate, who truly has not lacked occasion to recognize what he is and what he must be, still did not want to be a Jew, as decades ago, when I wore white half socks and leather breeches and nervously eyed myself in the mirror, hoping it would show me an impressive German youth? Naturally not. The foolishness of my masquerading in Austrian dress—although it was, after all, part of my heritage—belongs to the distant past. It is all right with me that I was not a German youth and am not a German man. No matter how the disguise may have looked on me, it now lies in the attic. If today discomfort arises in me when a Jew takes it for granted, legitimately, that I am part of his community, then it is not because I don't want to be a Jew, but only because I cannot be one. And yet must be one. And I do not merely submit to this necessity, but expressly claim it as part of my person. The necessity and impossibility of being a Jew, that is what causes me indistinct pain. It is with this necessity, this impossibility, this oppression, this inability that I must deal here, and in doing so I can only hope, without certainty,

82

that my individual story is exemplary enough also to reach those who neither are nor have to be Jews.

First of all, concerning the impossibility. If being a Jew means sharing a religious creed with other Jews, participating in Jewish cultural and family tradition, cultivating a Jewish national ideal, then I find myself in a hopeless situation. I don't believe in the God of Israel. I know very little about Jewish culture. I see myself as a boy at Christmas, plodding through a snow-covered village to midnight mass; I don't see myself in a synagogue. I hear my mother appealing to Jesus, Mary, and Joseph when a minor household misfortune occurred; I hear no adjuration of the Lord in Hebrew. The picture of my father—whom I hardly knew, since he remained where his Kaiser had sent him and his fatherland deemed him to be in the safest care—did not show me a bearded Jewish sage, but rather a Tyrolean Imperial Rifleman in the uniform of the First World War. I was nineteen years old when I heard of the existence of a Yiddish language, although on the other hand I knew full well that my religiously and ethnically very mixed family was regarded by the neighbors as Jewish, and that no one in my home thought of denying or hiding what was unconcealable anyhow. I was a Jew, just as one of my schoolmates was the son of a bankrupt innkeeper: when the boy was alone the financial ruin of his family may have meant next to nothing to him, when he joined us others he retreated, as we did, into resentful embarrassment.

If being a Jew implies having a cultural heritage or religious ties, then I was not one and can never become one. Certainly, it could be argued that a heritage can be acquired, ties established, and that therefore to be a Jew could be a matter of a voluntary decision. Who would possibly prevent me from learning the Hebrew language, from reading Jewish history and tales, and from participating—even without belief—in Jewish ritual, which is both religious and national? Well supplied with all the requisite knowledge of Jewish culture from the prophets to Martin Buber, I could emigrate to Israel and call myself Yochanan. I have the freedom to choose to be a Jew, and this freedom is my very personal and universally human privilege. That is what I am assured of.

But do I really have it? I don't believe so. Would Yochanan, the proud bearer of a new self-acquired identity, be made immune on the 24th of December by his supposedly thorough knowledge of chassidism against thoughts of a Christmas tree with gilded nuts? Would the upright Israeli, conversing fluently in Hebrew, be able so completely to obliterate the white-stockinged youth who once took such pains to speak a local dialect? In modern literature the switch of identity is quite a stimulating game, but in my case it is a challenge that one meets with no certainty of success, in one's human totality, without the chance of an interim solution, and would—it seems to me—be wholly predestined to fail. One can reestablish the link with a tradition that one has lost, but one cannot freely invent it for oneself, that is the problem. Since I was not a Jew, I am not one; and since I am not one, I won't be able to become one. A Yochanan on Mt. Carmel, haunted and spirited home by memories of Alpine valleys and folk rituals, would be even more inauthentic than was once the youth with his knee socks. To be who one is by becoming the person one should be and wants to be: for me this dialectical process of self-realization is obstructed. Because being Something, not as metaphysical essence, but as the simple summation of early experience, absolutely has priority. Everyone must be who he was in the first years of his life, even if later these were buried under. No one can become what he cannot find in his memories.

Thus I am not permitted to be a Jew. But since all the same I must be one and since this compulsion excludes the possibilities that might allow me to be something other than a Jew, can I not find myself at all? Must I acquiesce, without a past, as a shadow of the universal-abstract (which does not exist) and take refuge in the empty phrase that I am simply a human being? But patience, we haven't reached that point yet. Since the necessity exists—and how compelling it is!—perhaps the impossibility can be resolved. After all, one wants to live without hiding, as I did when I was in the underground, and without dissolving into the abstract. A human being? Certainly, who would not want to be one. But you are a human being only if you are a German, a Frenchman, a Christian, a member of whatever identifiable social group. I must be a Jew and will be one, with or without religion, within or outside a tradition, whether as Jean, Hans, or Yochanan. Why I must be one is what will be told here.

It didn't begin when schoolmates said to the boy: You're Jews anyway. Nor with the fight on the ramp of the university, during which, long before Hitler's ascent to power, a Nazi fist knocked out one of my teeth. Yes, we are Jews, and what of it? I answered my schoolmate. Today my tooth, tomorrow yours, and the devil take you, I thought to myself after the beating, and bore the gap proudly like an interesting duelling scar.

It didn't begin until 1935, when I was sitting over a newspaper in a Vienna coffeehouse and was studying the Nuremberg Laws, which had just been enacted across the border in Germany. I needed only to skim them and already I could perceive that they applied to me. Society, concretized in the National Socialist German state, which the world recognized absolutely as the legitimate representative of the German people, had just made me formally and beyond any question a Jew, or rather it had given a new dimension to what I had already known earlier, but which at the time was of no great consequence to me, namely, that I was a Jew.

What sort of new dimension? Not one that was immediately fathomable. After I had read the Nuremberg Laws I was no more Jewish than a half hour before. My features had not become more Mediterranean-Semitic, my frame of reference had not suddenly been filled by magic power with Hebrew allusions, the Christmas tree had not wondrously transformed itself into the seven-armed candelabra. If the sentence that society had passed on me had a tangible meaning, it could only be that henceforth I was a quarry of Death. Well, sooner or later it claims all of us. But the Jew—and I now was one by decree of law and society—was more firmly promised to death, already in the midst of life. His days were a period of false grace that could be revoked at any second. I do not believe that I am inadmissibly projecting Auschwitz and the Final Solution back to 1935 when I advance these thoughts today. Rather, I am certain that in that year, at that moment when I read the Laws, I did indeed already hear the death threat—better, the death sentence—and certainly no special sensitivity toward history was required for that. Had I not already heard a hundred times the appeal to fate—coupled with the call for Germany's awakening—that the Jew should perish? "Juda verrecke!" —that was something completely different than the almost cheerful "L'aristocrat, à la laterne!" Even if one did not consider or did not know that historically it linked up with countless pogroms of the past, it was not a revolutionary clamor, but rather the carefully considered demand of a people, compressed into a slogan, a war cry! Also in those same days I had once seen in a German magazine the photo of a Winter Relief event in a Rhenish town, and in the foreground, in front of the tree gleaming with electric lights, there was proudly displayed a banner with the text: "No one shall go hungry, no one shall freeze, but the Jews shall die like dogs." And only three years later, on the day of Austria's incorporation into the *Grossdeutsches Reich,* I heard Joseph Goebbels screaming on the radio that one really ought not to make such a fuss about the fact that in Vienna a few Jews were now committing suicide.

To be a Jew, that meant for me, from this moment on, to be a dead man on leave, someone to be murdered, who only by chance was not yet where he properly belonged; and so it has remained, in many variations, in various degrees of intensity, until today. The death threat, which I felt for the first time with complete clarity while reading the Nuremberg Laws, included what is commonly referred to as the methodic "degradation" of the Jews by the Nazis. Formulated differently: the denial of human dignity sounded the death threat. Daily, for years on end, we could read and hear that we were lazy, evil, ugly, capable only of misdeed, clever only to the extent that we pulled one over on others. We were incapable of founding a state, but also by no means suited to assimilate with our host nations. By their very presence, our bodies—hairy, fat, and bow-legged—befouled public swimming pools, yes, even park benches. Our hideous faces, depraved and spoilt by protruding ears and hanging noses, were disgusting to our fellow men, fellow citizens of yesterday. We were not worthy of love and thus also not of life. Our sole right, our sole duty was to disappear from the face of the earth.

The degradation of the Jews was, I am convinced, identical with the death threat long before Auschwitz. In this regard Jean-Paul Sartre, already in 1946 in his book *Anti-Semite and Jew,* offered a few perceptions that are still valid today. There is no "Jewish Problem," he said, only a problem of antisemitism; the antisemite forced the Jew into a situation in which he permitted his enemy to stamp him with a self-image. Both points appear to me to be unassailable. But in his short phenomenological sketch Sartre could not describe the total, crushing force of antisemitism, a force that had brought the Jew to that point, quite aside from the fact that the great author himself probably did not comprehend it in its entire overwhelming might. The Jew—and Sartre speaks here, without making a value judgment, of the "inauthentic" Jew, that is, the Jew who has fallen victim to the myth of the "universal man"—subjugates himself, in his flight from the Jewish fate, to the power of his oppressor. But one must say in his favor that in the years of the Third Reich the Jew stood with his back to the wall, and it too was hostile. There was no way out. Because it was not only radical Nazis, officially certified by the party, who denied that we were worthy of being loved and thereby worthy of life. All of Germany—but what am I saying!—the whole world nodded its head in approval of the undertaking, even if here and there with a certain superficial regret.

One must remember: when after World War II streams of refugees poured out of the various communist-ruled lands into the West, the countries of the proclaimed free world outdid one another in their willingness to grant asylum and aid, although among all the emigrants there was only a handful whose lives would have been directly threatened in their homeland. But even when it long since should have been clear to any discerning person what awaited us in the German Reich, no one wanted to have us. Thus, it necessarily had to reach the point where the Jews, whether authentic or not, whether secure in the illusion of a God and a national hope, or assimilated, found within themselves no powers of resistance when their enemy burned the image from Streicher's *Stürmer* into their skin. It should be noted that this weakness had only little to do with the classical Jewish self-hatred of those German Jews of the time before the outbreak of Nazism who were not only willing but craving to assimilate. The self-haters had believed that they were unable to be what they so much wanted to be: Germans, and therefore they rejected themselves. They had not wanted to accept their existence as non-Germans, but no one had forced them to reject themselves as Jews. When, on the other hand, between 1933 and 1945 precisely the brightest and most upright Jewish minds, authentic or inauthentic, capitulated to Streicher, that was a wholly different act of resignation, no longer moral, but rather social and philosophic in nature. This, so they must have told themselves, is how the world sees us, as lazy, ugly, useless, and evil; in view of such universal agreement what sense does it still make to object and say that we *are* not that way! The surrender of the Jews to the *Stürmer* image of themselves was nothing other than the acknowledgment of a social reality. To oppose it with a self-evaluation based on other standards at times had to appear ridiculous or mad.

In order to discuss it, however, one must have experienced it. When I think about the social reality of the wall of rejection that arose before us everywhere, my stay in Auschwitz-Monowitz comes to mind. In the camp itself, but also among the so-called free workers at the worksite, there was a strict ethnic hierarchy, imposed by the Nazis on all of us. A German from the Reich was regarded more highly than a German from an Eastern country. A Flemish Belgian was worth more than a Walloon. A Ukrainian from occupied Poland ranked higher than his Polish compatriot. A forced laborer from Eastern Europe was more poorly regarded than an Italian. Far down on the bottom rungs of the ladder were the concentration camp inmates, and among them, in turn, the Jews had the lowest rank. There was not a single non-Jewish professional criminal, no matter how degenerate he may have been, who did not stand high above us. The Poles, whether they were genuine freedom fighters who had been thrown into the camp after the ill-fated Warsaw insurrection, or merely small-time pickpockets, despised us unanimously. So did half-illiterate White Russian workers. But also Frenchmen. I still hear a free French worker conversing with a Jewish-French concentration camp inmate: "I'm French," the inmate said. "Français, toi? Mais, tu es juif, mon ami," his countryman retorted objectively and without hostility; for in a mixture of fear and indifference he had absorbed the teachings of Europe's German masters. I repeat: the world approved of the place to which the Germans had assigned us, the small world of the camp and the wide world outside, which but rarely, in individual heroic instances, arose in protest when we were taken at night from our homes in Vienna or Berlin, in Amsterdam, Paris, or Brussels.

The degradation proceedings directed against us Jews, which began with the proclamation of the Nuremberg Laws and as a direct result led all the way to Treblinka, met on our, on my side with an equivalent proceedings aimed at the reattainment of dignity. For me, until today, this case is not closed. Let my endeavor to gain clarity concerning its stages and its preliminary result be recorded here, and permit me to request of the reader that he accompany me awhile along this path. It is short, but difficult to tread, and full of obstacles and traps. For what, after all, actually is the nature of the dignity that was first denied me in 1935, officially withheld from me until 1945, and that perhaps even today one does not want to grant me, and that I must therefore attain through my own effort? What is dignity, really?

One can try to answer by inverting the above-formulated identifica-

tion of degradation and death threat. If I was correct that the deprivation
of dignity was nothing other than the potential deprivation of life, then
dignity would have to be the right to live. If it was also correct when I
said that the granting and depriving of dignity are acts of social agreement, sentences against which there is no appeal on the grounds of one's
"self-understanding," so that it would be senseless to argue against the
social body that deprives us of our dignity with the claim that we do indeed "feel" worthy—if all of this were valid, then every effort to regain
our dignity would have been of no value, and it would still be so today.
Degradation, that is, living under the threat of death, would be an in-
escapable fate. But luckily, things are not entirely the way this logic
claims. It is certainly true that dignity can be bestowed only by society,
whether it be the dignity of some office, a professional or, very generally
speaking, civil dignity; and the merely individual, subjective claim ("I am
a human being and as such I have my dignity, no matter what you may do
or say!") is an empty academic game, or madness. Still, the degraded person, threatened with death, is able—and here we break through the logic
of the final sentencing—to convince society of his dignity by taking his
fate upon himself and at the same time rising in revolt against it.

The first step must be the unqualified recognition that the verdict of
the social group is a given reality. When I read the Nuremberg Laws in
1935 and realized not only that they applied to me but also that they were
the expression, concentrated in legal-textual form, of the verdict "Death
to the Jews!" which already earlier had been pronounced by German society, I could have taken intellectual flight, turned on the defense me-
chanisms, and thereby have lost my case for rehabilitation. Then I would
have told myself: well, well, so this is the will of the National Socialist
state, of the German *pays légal*; but it has nothing to do with the real
Germany, the *pays réel*, which has no thought whatever of ostracizing
me. Or I could have argued that it was only Germany, a land unfortunately sinking into a bloody madness, that was so absurdly stamping me as
subhuman (in the literal sense of the word), whereas to my good fortune
the great wide world outside, in which there are Englishmen, Frenchmen,
Americans, and Russians, is immune to the collective paranoia scourging
Germany. Or finally, even if I had abandoned the illusion both of a
German *pays réel* and of a world immune against the German mental disorder, I could have comforted myself with the thought: no matter what

they say about me, it isn't true. I am true only as I see and understand
myself deep within; I am what I am for myself and in myself, and nothing
else.

I am not saying that now and then I did not succumb to such temptation. I can only testify that finally I learned to resist it and that already at
that time, in 1935, I vaguely felt the necessity to convince the world of my
dignity, the world that by no means indignantly and unanimously broke
off all relations with the Third Reich. I understood, even if unclearly, that
while I had to accept the verdict as such, I could force the world to revise
it. I accepted the judgment of the world, with the decision to overcome it
through revolt.

Revolt; well, of course, that is another one of those high-sounding
words. It could lead the reader to believe that I was a hero or that I
falsely want to present myself as one. I certainly was no hero. When the
little grey Volkswagen with the POL license plate crossed my path, first
in Vienna, then in Brussels, I was so afraid that I couldn't breathe. When
the Kapo drew back his arm to strike me, I didn't stand firm like a cliff,
but ducked. And still, I tried to initiate proceedings to regain my dignity,
and beyond physical survival that provided me with just the slightest
chance to survive the nightmare morally also. There is not much that I
can present in my favor, but let it be noted anyhow. I took it upon myself
to be a Jew, even though there would have been possibilities for a com-
promise settlement. I joined a resistance movement whose prospects for
success were very dim. Also, I finally relearned what I and my kind often
had forgotten and what was more crucial than the moral power to resist:
to hit back.

Before me I see the prisoner foreman Juszek, a Polish professional
criminal of horrifying vigor. In Auschwitz he once hit me in the face because of a trifle; that is how he was used to dealing with all the Jews under
his command. At this moment—I felt it with piercing clarity—it was up
to me to go a step further in my prolonged appeals case against society.
In open revolt I struck Juszek in the face in turn. My human dignity lay
in this punch to his jaw—and that it was in the end I, the physically much
weaker man, who succumbed and was woefully thrashed, meant nothing
to me. Painfully beaten, I was satisfied with myself. But not, as one might
think, for reasons of courage and honor, but only because I had grasped
well that there are situations in life in which our body is our entire self

and our entire fate. I was my body and nothing else: in hunger, in the blow that I suffered, in the blow that I dealt. My body, debilitated and crusted with filth, was my calamity. My body, when it tensed to strike, was my physical and metaphysical dignity. In situations like mine, physical violence is the sole means for restoring a disjointed personality. In the punch, I was myself—for myself and for my opponent. What I later read in Frantz Fanon's *Les damnés de la terre*, in a theoretical analysis of the behavior of colonized peoples, I anticipated back then when I gave concrete social form to my dignity by punching a human face. To be a Jew meant the acceptance of the death sentence imposed by the world as a world verdict. To flee before it by withdrawing into one's self would have been nothing but a disgrace, whereas acceptance was simultaneously the physical revolt against it. I became a person not by subjectively appealing to my abstract humanity but by discovering myself within the given social reality as a rebelling Jew and by realizing myself as one.

The proceedings, I said, went on and still go on. At present, I have neither won nor lost the case. After the collapse of the National Socialist Reich there was a brief global hour in which I was able to believe that from the bottom up everything was transformed. For a short time in those days I was able to foster the illusion that my dignity was totally restored, through my own, no matter how modest, activity in the resistance movement, through the heroic uprising in the Warsaw Ghetto, but above all through the contempt that the world showed toward those who had stripped me of my dignity. I could believe that the deprivation of dignity that we had experienced had been a historical error, an aberration, a collective sickness of the world, from which the latter had recovered at the moment when in Reims German generals signed the declaration of surrender in the presence of Eisenhower. Soon I learned worse. In Poland and in the Ukraine, while they were still discovering Jewish mass graves, there were antisemitic disturbances. In France the ever sickly petty bourgeoisie had allowed itself to be infected by the occupiers. When survivors and refugees returned and demanded their old dwellings, it happened that simple housewives, in a peculiar mixture of satisfaction and chagrin, said: "Tiens, ils reviennent, on ne les a tout de même tué." Even in countries that previously had hardly known any antisemitism, as in Holland, there suddenly existed as a relict of the German propaganda a "Jewish Problem," though scarcely any more Jews. England barred its Mandate of

Palestine to those Jews who had escaped from the camps and jails and who tried to immigrate. In a very short time I was forced to recognize that little had changed, that I was still the man condemned to be murdered in due time, even though the potential executioner now cautiously restrained himself or, at best, even loudly protested his disapproval of what had happened.

I understood reality. But should this perhaps have occasioned me to come to grips with the problem of antisemitism? Not at all. Antisemitism and the Jewish Question, as historical, socially determined conceptual phenomena, were not and are not any concern of mine. They are entirely a matter for the antisemites, their disgrace or their sickness. The antisemites have something to overcome, not I. I would play into their unclean hands if I began investigating what share religious, economic, or other factors have in the persecution of the Jews. If I were to engage in such investigations I would only be falling for the intellectual dupery of so-called historical objectivity, according to which the murdered are as guilty as the murderers, if not even more guilty. A wound was inflicted on me. I must disinfect and bind it, not contemplate why the ruffian raised his club, and, through the inferred "That's Why," in the end partly absolve him.

It was not the antisemites who concerned me, it was only with my own existence that I had to cope. That was hard enough. Certain possibilities, which had emerged for me in the war years, no longer existed. From 1945 to 1947 I could not very well sew on a yellow star without appearing foolish or eccentric to myself. There also was no longer any opportunity to punch the enemy in his face, for he was not so easy to recognize anymore. The reattainment of dignity, just as urgent as in the previous years of war and National Socialism, but now—in a climate of deceptive peace—infinitely more difficult, remained a compulsion and desire. Except that I had to recognize even more clearly than in the days when physical revolt was at least possible that I was confronted with necessity and impossibility.

At this point I must stop for a moment and separate myself from all those Jews who do not speak from the realm of my own experience. In his book *La condition réflexive de l'homme juif* the French philosopher Robert Misrahi said: "The Nazi Holocaust is henceforth the absolute and radical reference point for the existence of every Jew." That is not to be doubted, yet I am convinced that not every Jew is capable of thinking out this relationship. Only those who have lived through a fate like mine, and no one else, can refer their lives to the years 1933–45. By no means do I say this with pride. It would be ridiculous enough to boast of something that one did not do but only underwent. Rather it is with a certain shame that I assert my sad privilege and suggest that while the Holocaust is truly the existential reference point for all Jews, only we, the sacrificed, are able to spiritually relive the catastrophic event as it was or fully picture it as it could be again. Let others not be prevented from empathizing. Let them contemplate a fate that yesterday could have been and tomorrow can be theirs. Their intellectual efforts will meet with our respect, but it will be a sceptical one, and in conversation with them we will soon grow silent and say to ourselves: go ahead, good people, trouble your heads as much as you want; you still sound like a blind man talking about color.

The parentheses are now closed. I am once again alone with myself and a few good comrades. I find myself in the postwar years, which no longer permitted any of us to react with violence to something that refused to reveal itself clearly to us. Again I see myself confronted with necessity and impossibility.

That this impossibility does not apply to all is obvious. Among the Jews of this time, whether they be workers in Kiev, storekeepers in Brooklyn, or farmers in the Negev, there are enough men and women for whom being a Jew was and always remained a positive fact. They speak Yiddish or Hebrew. They celebrate the sabbath. They explicate the Talmud or stand at attention as young soldiers under the blue-and-white banner with the Star of David. Whether religiously or nationally or merely in personal reverence before the picture of their grandfather with his sidelocks, they are *Jews* as members of a community. One could briefly digress perhaps and, together with the sociologist Georges Friedmann, ask the secondary question of whether their progeny will still be Jews and whether the end of the Jewish people may not be imminent in that Mediterranean country where the Israeli is already displacing the Jew, as well as in the Diaspora, where perhaps the total assimilation of the Jews—not so much to their host peoples, who for their part are losing their national character, but to the larger unity of the technical-industrial world—could take place.

I'll not pursue this question further. The existence or the disappearance of the Jewish people as an ethnic-religious community does not excite me. In my deliberations I am unable to consider Jews who are Jews because they are sheltered by tradition. I can speak solely for myself—and, even if with caution, for contemporaries, probably numbering into the millions, whose being Jewish burst upon them with elemental force, and who must stand this test without God, without history, without messianic-national hope. For them, for me, being a Jew means feeling the tragedy of yesterday as an inner oppression. On my left forearm I bear the Auschwitz number; it reads more briefly than the Pentateuch or the Talmud and yet provides more thorough information. It is also more binding than basic formulas of Jewish existence. If to myself and the world, including the religious and nationally minded Jews, who do not regard me as one of their own, I say: I am a Jew, then I mean by that those realities and possibilities that are summed up in the Auschwitz number.

In the two decades that have passed since my liberation I have gradually come to realize that it does not matter whether an existence can be positively defined. Sartre had already said once that a Jew is a person who is regarded by others as a Jew, and later Max Frisch dramatically portrayed this in *Andorra*. This view does not need to be corrected, but perhaps one may amplify it. For even if the others do not decide that I am a Jew, as they did with the poor devil in *Andorra*, who would have liked to become a carpenter and whom they permitted only to be a merchant, I am still a Jew by the mere fact that the world around me does not expressly designate me as a non-Jew. To be something can mean that one is *not* something else. As a Non-non-Jew, I am a Jew; I must be one and must want to be one. I must accept this and affirm it in my daily existence, whether —showing my colors—I butt into a conversation when stupid things are said about Jews at the greengrocery, whether I address an unknown audience on the radio, or whether I write for a magazine.

But since being a Jew not only means that I bear within me a catastrophe that occurred yesterday and cannot be ruled out for tomorrow, it is —beyond being a duty—also *fear*. Every morning when I get up I can read the Auschwitz number on my forearm, something that touches the deepest and most closely intertwined roots of my existence; indeed I am not even sure if this is not my entire existence. Then I feel approximately as I did back then when I got a taste of the first blow from a policeman's fist. Every day anew I lose my trust in the world. The Jew without positive determinants, the Catastrophe Jew, as we will unhesitatingly call him, must get along without trust in the world. My neighbor greets me in a friendly fashion, *Bonjour, Monsieur;* I doff my hat, *Bonjour, Madame.* But Madame and Monsieur are separated by interstellar distances; for yesterday a Madame looked away when they led off a Monsieur, and through the barred windows of the departing car a Monsieur viewed a Madame as if she were a stone angel from a bright and stern heaven, which is forever closed for the Jew. I read an official announcement in which "la population" is called upon to do something or other, told that the trash cans are to be put out on time or that the flag is to be displayed on a national holiday. *La population.* Still another one of those unearthly realms that I can enter as little as I can Kafka's castle; for yesterday "la population" had great fear of hiding me, and whether tomorrow it would have more courage if I knocked at the door, unfortunately is not certain.

Twenty years have passed since the Holocaust. Glorious years for such as us. Nobel prize winners in abundance. There were French presidents named René Mayer and Pierre Mendès-France; an American UN delegate by the name of Goldberg practices a most dignified anticommunist American patriotism. I don't trust this peace. Declarations of human rights, democratic constitutions, the free world and the free press, nothing can again lull me into the slumber of security from which I awoke in 1935. As a Jew I go through life like a sick man with one of those ailments that cause no great hardships but are certain to end fatally. He didn't always suffer from that sickness. When he attempts, like Peer Gynt, to peel his self out of the onion, he doesn't discover the malady. His first walk to school, his first love, his first verses had nothing to do with it. But now he is a sick man, first and foremost and more deeply than he is a tailor, a bookkeeper, or a poet. Thus, I too am precisely what I am not, because I did not exist until I became it, above all else: a Jew. Death, from which the sick man will be unable to escape, is what threatens me. *Bonjour, Madame, Bonjour, Monsieur,* they greet each other. But she cannot and will not relieve her sick neighbor of his mortal illness at the cost of suffering to death from it herself. And so they remain strangers to one another.

Without trust in the world I face my surroundings as a Jew who is alien and alone, and all that I can manage is to get along within my foreignness. I must accept being foreign as an essential element of my personality, insist upon it as if upon an inalienable possession. Still and each day anew I find myself alone. I was unable to force yesterday's murderers and tomorrow's potential aggressors to recognize the moral truth of their crimes, because the world, in its totality, did not help me to do it. Thus I am alone, as I was when they tortured me. Those around me do not appear to me as antihumans, as did my former torturers; they are my co-humans, not affected by me and the danger prowling at my side. I pass them with a greeting and without hostility. I cannot rely on them, only on a Jewish identity that is without positive determinants, my burden and my support.

Where there is a common bond between me and the world, whose still unrevoked death sentence I acknowledge as a social reality, it dissolves in polemics. You don't want to listen? Listen anyhow. You don't want to know to where your indifference can again lead you and me at any time? I'll tell you. What happened is no concern of yours because you didn't know, or were too young, or not even born yet? You should have seen, and your youth gives you no special privilege, and break with your father.

Once again I must ask myself the question that I already raised fleetingly in my essay "Resentments": am I perhaps mentally ill and am I not suffering from an incurable ailment, from hysteria? The question is merely rhetorical. I have long since provided myself with a fully conclusive answer. I know that what oppresses me is no neurosis, but rather precisely reflected reality. Those were no hysteric hallucinations when I heard the Germans call for the Jews to "die like a dog!" and, in passing, heard how people said that there really must be something suspicious about the Jews, because otherwise they would hardly be treated so severely. "They are being arrested, so they must have done something," said a proper social-democratic worker's wife in Vienna. "How horrible, what they are doing with the Jews, *mais enfin . . .*," speculated a humane and patriotic-minded man in Brussels. I am thus forced to conclude that I am not deranged and was not deranged, but rather that the neurosis is on the part of the historical occurrence. The others are the madmen, and I am left standing around helplessly among them, a fully sane person who joined a tour through a psychiatric clinic and suddenly lost sight of the doctors and orderlies. But since the sentence passed on me by the madmen can, after all, be carried out at any moment, it is totally binding, and my own mental lucidity is entirely irrelevant.

These reflections are nearing their end. Now that I have explained how I manage in this world, it is time to testify how I relate to my kins-men, the Jews. But are they really related to me after all? Whatever an ethnologist may determine—for example, that my external appearance presents one or another Jewish characteristic—may be relevant if I land in a screaming mob that is hounding Jews. It loses all significance when I am alone or among Jews. Do I have a Jewish nose? That could become a calamity if a pogrom breaks out again. But that does not align me with a single other Jewish nose anywhere. The Jewish appearance that I may or may not have—I don't know if I do—is a matter for the others and be-comes my concern only in the objective relationship they establish toward me. If I were to look like I had stepped out of Johann von Leers's book *Juden sehen euch an*[15] it would have no subjective reality for me; it would, to be sure, establish a community of fate, but no positive community between me and my fellow Jews. Thus there remains only the intellectual —more correctly, the consciously perceived—relationship of Jews, Juda-ism, and myself.

That it is a nonrelationship I have already stated at the outset. With Jews as Jews I share practically nothing: no language, no cultural tradi-tion, no childhood memories. In the Austrian region of Vorarlberg there was an innkeeper and butcher of whom I was told that he spoke fluent Hebrew. He was my great-grandfather. I never saw him and it must be nearly a hundred years since he died. Before the Holocaust my interest in Jewish things and Jews was so slight that with the best of intentions I could not say today which of my acquaintances at that time was a Jew and which was not. However I might try to find in Jewish history my own past, in Jewish culture my own heritage, in Jewish folklore my personal recollections, the result would be nil. The environment in which I had lived in the years when one acquires one's self was not Jewish, and that cannot be reversed. But the fruitlessness of the search for my Jewish self by no means stands as a barrier between me and my solidarity with every threatened Jew in this world.

I read in the paper that in Moscow they discovered an illegally op-erating bakery for unleavened Jewish Passover bread and arrested the bakers. As a means of nourishment the ritual *matzoth* of the Jews interest me somewhat less than rye crisps. Nevertheless, the action of the Soviet authorities fills me with uneasiness, indeed with indignation. Some Amer-ican country club, so I hear, does not accept Jews as members. Not for the

world would I wish to belong to this obviously dismal middle-class association, but the cause of the Jews who demand permission to join becomes
mine. That some Arab statesman calls for Israel to be wiped off the map
cuts me to the quick, even though I have never visited the state of Israel
and do not feel the slightest inclination to live there. My solidarity with
every Jew whose freedom, equal rights, or perhaps even physical existence
is threatened is *also*, but *not only*, a reaction to antisemitism, which,
according to Sartre, is not an opinion but the predisposition and readiness
to commit the crime of genocide. This solidarity is part of my person and
a weapon in the battle to regain my dignity. Without being a Jew in the
sense of a positive identification, it is not until I am a Jew in the recognition and acknowledgment of the world verdict on the Jews and not until
I finally participate in the historical appeals process that I may speak of
freedom.

Solidarity in the face of threat is all that links me with my Jewish
contemporaries, the believers as well as the nonbelievers, the national-
minded as well as those ready to assimilate. For them that is perhaps little
or nothing at all. For me and my continued existence it means much, more
probably than my appreciation of Proust's books or my affection for the
stories of Schnitzler or my joy in seeing the Flemish landscape. Without
Proust and Schnitzler and the wind-bent poplars at the North Sea I would
be poorer than I am, but I would still be human. Without the feeling of
belonging to the threatened I would be a self-surrendering fugitive from
reality.

I say reality, with emphasis, because in the end that is what matters
to me. Antisemitism, which made a Jew of me, may be a form of madness;
that is not what is in question here. Whether it is a madness or not, it is
in any event a historical and social fact. I was, after all, really in Auschwitz
and not in Himmler's imagination. And antisemitism is still a reality; only
someone with complete social and historical blindness could deny it. It is
a reality in its core countries, Austria and Germany, where Nazi war
criminals either are not convicted or receive ridiculously mild prison sentences, of which for the most part they serve hardly a third. It is a reality
in England and the United States, where one tolerates the Jews, but
would not be unhappy to be rid of them. It is a reality, and with what dire
consequences, in the spiritual global domain of the Catholic Church. The
complexity and confusion of the Vatican Council's consultations on the

so-called Declaration on the Jews were, despite the honorable effort of so many a prelate, grievously shameful.

It may well be—but in view of the given circumstances one can by no means count on it—that in the Nazi death factories the final act was played in the vast historical drama of Jewish persecution. I believe that the dramaturgy of antisemitism continues to exist. A new mass extermination of Jews cannot be ruled out as a possibility. What would happen if in a war against the small land of Israel the Arab countries, today supported by arms shipments from East and West, were to gain a total victory? What would an America that had come under the sway of military fascism mean not only for the Negroes but also for the Jews? What would the fate of the Jews have been in France, the European country with their greatest number, if at the beginning of this decade not de Gaulle had triumphed, but the OAS?

With some reluctance I read in the study of a very young Dutch Jew the following definition of the Jew: "A Jew can be described as someone who has more fear, mistrust, and vexation than his fellow citizens who were never persecuted." The apparently correct definition is rendered false by the absence of an indispensable extension, which would have to read: ". . . for with good reason he awaits a new catastrophe at any moment." The awareness of the last cataclysm and the legitimate fear of a new one is what it all amounts to. I, who bear both within me—and the latter with double weight, since it was only by chance that I escaped the former—am not "traumatized," but rather my spiritual and psychic condition corresponds completely to reality. The consciousness of my being a Holocaust Jew is not an ideology. It may be compared to the class consciousness that Marx tried to reveal to the proletarians of the nineteenth century. I experienced in my existence and exemplify through it a historical reality of my epoch, and since I experienced it more deeply than most other Jews, I can also shed more light on it. That is not to my credit and not because I am so wise, but only because of the chance of fate.

Everything could be borne more easily if my bond with other Jews were not limited to the solidarity of revolt, if the necessity did not constantly run up against the impossibility. I know it only too well: I was sitting next to a Jewish friend at a performance of Arnold Schönberg's "A Survivor From Warsaw" when, accompanied by the sounds of trumpets, the chorus intoned the words "Sch'ma Israel"; my friend turned as white as chalk and beads of perspiration appeared on his brow. My heart did not beat faster, yet I felt myself to be more wanting than my comrade, whom the Jewish prayer, sung to the blasts of trumpets, had powerfully affected. To be a deeply stirred Jew, I thought to myself afterwards, is not possible for me, I can be a Jew only in fear and anger, when—in order to attain dignity—fear transforms itself into anger. "Hear, oh Israel" is not my concern. Only a "hear, oh world" wants angrily to break out from within me. The six-digit number on my forearm demands it. That is what the awareness of catastrophe, the dominant force of my existence, requires.

Often I have asked myself whether one can live humanly in the tension between fear and anger. Those who have followed these deliberations may well see their author as a monster, if not of vengeance, then at least of bitterness. There may be a trace of truth in such a judgment, but only a trace. Whoever attempts to be a Jew in my way and under the conditions imposed on me, whoever hopes, by clarifying his own Holocaust-determined existence, to draw together and shape within himself the reality of the so-called Jewish Question, is wholly void of naïveté. Honey-sweet humane pronouncements do not flow from his lips. He is not good at gestures of magnanimity. But this does not mean that fear and anger condemn him to be less righteous than his ethically inspired contemporaries are. He is able to have friends and he has them, even among members of just those nations who hung him forever on the torture hook between fear and anger. He can also read books and listen to music as do the uninjured, and with no less feeling than they. If moral questions are involved, he will probably prove to be more sensitive to injustice of every kind than his fellow man. He will certainly react more excitably to a photo of club-swinging South African policemen or American sheriffs who sick howling dogs on black civil rights protesters. Because it became hard for me to be a human being does not mean that I have become a monster.

In the end, nothing else differentiates me from the people among whom I pass my days than a vague, sometimes more, sometimes less perceptible restiveness. But it is a *social* unrest, not a metaphysical one. It is not Being that oppresses me, or Nothingness, or God, or the Absence of God, only society. For it and only it caused the disturbance in my existential balance, which I am trying to oppose with an upright gait. It and only it robbed me of my trust in the world. Metaphysical distress is a fashionable concern of the highest standing. Let it remain a matter for those who have always known who and what they are, why they are that way, and that they are permitted to remain so. I must leave it to them—and it is not for that reason that I feel needy in their presence.

In my incessant effort to explore the basic condition of being a victim, in conflict with the necessity to be a Jew and the impossibility of being one, I believe to have recognized that the most extreme expectations and demands directed at us are of a physical and social nature. That such knowledge has made me unfit for profound and lofty speculation, I know. It is my hope that it has better equipped me to recognize reality.

TRANSLATORS' NOTES

1. The so-called Extremists Decree ("Radikalenerlass") was enacted in 1972 and intended to exclude from public service anyone whose constitutional disloyalty could be juridically demonstrated. Lack of both objective, democratic criteria and uniformity in application led to widespread opposition and, finally, partial reform.

2. The poem by Friedrich Hölderlin (1770–1843) is titled "Hälfte des Lebens" ("Life's Middle").

3. Heinrich von Kleist (1777–1811) ranks among the most significant German writers in the period between classicism and romanticism. The lines quoted are from his patriotic poem "Germania an ihre Kinder" ("Germania to her Children"), written in 1809, during the Napoleonic occupation.

4. Allusion to the existentialist philosopher Martin Heidegger (1889–1976), who stemmed from the Alemannic region of the southern Black Forest.

5. Janos Kadar; installed as head of Hungary's "Revolutionary Workers' and Peasants' Government" after the Soviets crushed the 1956 October uprising.

6. Friedrich Gottlieb Klopstock (1724–1803); the initiator of German poetic Irrationalism and *Erlebnisdichtung* ("poetry of experience"). Christoph Martin Wieland (1773–1813); together with Lessing, the outstanding representative of the German Enlightenment and a forerunner of German classicism.

7. Joseph von Eichendorff (1788–1857); romantic poet, recalled especially for his lyrics on nature and the theme of *Wanderlust*.

8. The images are contained in Goethe's poem "An den Mond" ("To the Moon"), which begins with the verses: "Again you fill copse and valley / With a misty sheen."

9. In the poem "Abendlied" ("Evening Song") the Swiss poet Gottfried Keller (1819–90) refers to his eyes—which afford him the "golden abundance of the world"—as his "dear little windows."

10. In the last stanza of Friedrich Nietzsche's poem "Vereinsamt" ("Alone"), the crows caw and fly with whirring wings toward the town. "Soon it will snow,— / Woe to him, who has no home!" the poem concludes.

11. Hans Friedrich Blunck (1888–1961); one of the most prominent authors of the Third Reich; from 1933 to 1935 he was president of the *Reichsschrifttumskammer*. Friedrich Griese (1890–1975); a Blood and Soil narrative writer and honored member of the National Socialist *Deutsche Akademie der Dichtung*.

12. "Du bist Orplid, mein Land" ("You are Orplid, my land") is the first line of the poem "Gesang Weylas" ("Weyla's Song") by Eduard Mörike (1804–75), the outstanding German lyric poet in the period between romanticism and realism.

13. Baron Karl von Stein (1757–1831); Prussian statesman, historian, political educator and reformer. Wilhelm Schäfer (1868–1952); particularly popular during the Nazi period for his novels and stories with strong thematic ties to the *Volk* and the German landscape. Member of the National Socialist *Deutsche Akademie der Dichtung*.

14. Matthias Claudius (1740–1815); lyric poet of simplicity, warmth, and deep humanity. His "Kriegslied" ("Song of War") begins with the stanza: " 'Tis war! 'Tis war! May Angels' fire / Speak against the shame. / 'Tis, mercy, war—and I desire / Not to have the blame!" Hermann Claudius (1878–   ); a great-grandson of Matthias Claudius, he regularly contributed poems tainted by Nazi ideology to the leading literary journal in Hitler's Germany, *Das innere Reich* (1933–44).

15. The racist diatribe *Juden sehen dich an* ("Jews Are Watching You") by the Nazi propagandist Johann von Leers (1902–   ) first appeared in 1933. (In his text, Améry has slightly misquoted the title.)

Jean Améry:
The Writer in Revolt

Jean Améry's suicide on October 17, 1978, ended a literary career that finds no parallel in postwar German letters, although it was determined by experiences that, unhappily, were not unique to him but were shared by scores of thousands. The victims of Nazism were countless, those who lived to bear testimony a handful. Améry, who withstood the years between 1938 and 1945 in exile, internment, hiding, and the inferno of the concentration camps, began his career late, and his time was severely measured. He was already fifty-four when this, his first book (originally entitled *Jenseits von Schuld und Sühne*, "Beyond Guilt and Atonement"), was published in 1966. Yet, in the space of a few years, the former Resistance member and Auschwitz survivor was able to establish himself among a discriminating audience as a political and cultural essayist-critic of unflinching moral courage, imposing intelligence and erudition, and stylistic brilliance. There is good reason to believe that he could have advanced to the very forefront of the German literary scene, had he been willing to abandon his solitary position of exile-in-permanence for an easier and, in concrete ways, more comfortable one closer to the mainstream of German intellectual activity. But such ambition did not, in fact, could not, entice him. Instead, he remained in Brussels, where he had found perilous cover after flight from his native Austria in 1938 and where he had returned after liberation from Bergen-Belsen in 1945. There he would exemplify through his person and his writing an uncompromising ethos of militant humanism within the estrangement that was his unalterable fate. In a series of essayistic autobiographical works, which began with *At the Mind's Limits*, he applied his moral and artistic vigor to an enlightenment of the human condition as it had manifested itself during the four decades of Western European intellectual and political history whose decisive reference point is the Nazi cataclysm.

In 1969 Améry expanded the autobiographical self-interrogation of *At the Mind's Limits* in an equally personal, relentlessly probing study, *Über das Altern* ("On Aging"), and three years later, in 1971, he published the most expressly autobiographical of his works, *Unmeisterliche Wanderjahre* (whose title alludes ironically to Goethe's Bildungsroman, *William Master's Journeyman Years*). Here, however, a word of clarification is due. For although the entirety of Jean Améry's major work is autobiographical, it does not yield a narrative of the external, factual data of his life but, by intention, a chronicle of his intellectual existence, which evolved in impassioned reaction to the philosophical and political turning points of an epoch that culminated in the monstrosity of the Third Reich.

Of the three books, *Unmeisterliche Wanderjahre* pursues the course of Améry's development most systematically—if this term is understood to describe a self-portrayal that is chronologically ordered but, for the rest, willfully subjective and strikingly artistic, a form of writing that Améry himself characterized as "a kind of autobiographical essayistic novel." In it, the reader accompanies him during his intellectual *Wanderjahre*, proceeding from an early German bourgeois-romantic irrationalism, by way of mind-sobering Viennese neopositivism, to self-liberation through the existentialist philosophy of his critically revered mentor, Sartre. Still later Améry became fervently preoccupied with structuralism, which, however, he excoriated as the most extreme form of dehumanization and autodestruction. In the end, devoid of all philosophical naïveté, mistrusting all manner of ideology, the radical humanist and, by his own designation, "Leftist Emotionalist" Améry resolutely affirmed a by-no-means secure or optimistic position on the side of man, heart, and practical democracy.

The chronology of *Unmeisterliche Wanderjahre* is conspicuously interrupted between the chapter "Debacle," which describes the collapse of the author's philosophical world, and the chapter "Trials of Existence," which takes up again in the postwar period. The missing years had already provided the raw material for At the Mind's Limits, whose origins the author alludes to briefly in his preface of 1966. In an edition of the book intended for readers who have no access to Améry's writing in German, it would seem appropriate to expand on this allusion and, beyond that, to offer approximately as much concrete biographical detail as he himself had chosen to disclose in the last years of a life in which the literary-intellectual enlightenment and transformation of external events held primacy over all impulses toward the purely personal.

The author was born in Vienna as Hans Meyer, the only child of a Catholic mother and a Jewish father, on October 31, 1912. His parents' home was in the Vorarlberg town of Hohenems, where his paternal forbears had lived since the seventeenth century. After his father's death in the First World War he moved with his mother to the resort town of Bad Ischl in the Salzkammergut, where she managed a livelihood as the proprietress of an inn while he attended the gymnasium in nearby Gmunden. Upon his graduation, mother and son moved again, now to Vienna. There Améry enrolled at the university, attending courses in philosophy and literature, but the necessity to work prevented the regular pursuit of his studies, and intermittently he held jobs as porter, messenger, bar pianist, and helper in book stores. At the same time, he was caught up in the political turmoil of the thirties that culminated in Austria's incorporation into the Third Reich. In Vienna, where antisemitism was rampant and Nazi sympathies ever on the increase, the fully assimilated Austrian Améry gradually recognized the significance of his Jewish identity, which, after the proclamation of the Nuremberg Laws in 1935, he regarded as personally binding. In 1937, against his mother's resistance, he married a young woman of Eastern European Jewish origin, a native of Graz in the Styria region. The following year they fled together from Austria to Belgium, an exile Améry's wife would not survive. She died of a heart ailment in Brussels at the age of twenty-eight, while he was captive in Auschwitz. His mother, who was not affected by the Nazi racial laws, remained in Vienna, where she died in 1939.

In 1940 Améry was arrested by the Belgians as a German alien and deported to southern France, where he was confined in various camps, among them the infamous Gurs camp in the Lower Pyrenees. He escaped from Gurs in 1941 and arduously made his way back to Belgium. What followed—work in the resistance movement, arrest and torture by the Gestapo in 1943—is depicted and explored in the second chapter of *At the Mind's Limits.* (Although Améry recovered fully from the injuries he had suffered in the torture cellar of Fort Breendonk, their psychic imprint remained indelible, and it was this phenomenon, the irrevocable loss of trust in the world, with all that accompanied it, that he was concerned to illuminate in his book.) The sequel to Améry's torture in Brussels was the renewed torture of Auschwitz. Once the Gestapo officers recognized that he was not the German military deserter they suspected him to be, they summarily condemned him to the horrors of the death camp.

After his liberation by the British in April 1945 Améry once again returned to Brussels, where he was to reside until his death. In order to support himself and his second wife—Maria Améry came originally from Vienna and had lived during the Hitler years in the United States—he turned to writing. Ever since he had published a schoolboy story in 1928, when he was sixteen, he had regarded writing as his vocation, but the trials he was subsequently to undergo prevented him from realizing a literary career. Now, amid the pervasive insecurity of exile-in-permanence, he was no longer able to view his literary bent as a calling but rather was compelled to ply his talent as a trade. For twenty years he refused to publish for a German audience (or to travel to Germany), and he maintained a free-lance literary existence through commissioned journalistic and other writing, exclusively for Swiss publications. The turning point came in 1964, when the German poet and critic Helmut Heissenbüttel, who had met Améry at a reading in Brussels, persuaded him to deliver a radio talk on the one subject that the former Gestapo prisoner and concentration camp survivor was willing to consider for any personal attempt at literary activity in Germany: Auschwitz, or, more exactly on that pivotal occasion, the "Encounter of the Intellectual with Auschwitz." This defiant beginning resulted in the book *At the Mind's Limits,* which soon founded Améry's reputation not only as one of the foremost contemporary German-language essayists but also as a moral spokesman for the victims of the Holocaust.

Améry's morality was not the result of any religious persuasion, something that was wholly foreign to him, nor of philosophical deliberation, in which he was thoroughly schooled, but rather of his own, very personal historical experience. As a victim, confronted with the immorality of history, he revolted against it, first as a member of the Resistance, then, after the war, as a writer-intellectual engagé, in the cause of his fellow victims and the threatened and injured individual altogether. Cast out from the German-language community by his fate during the Third Reich and later by his own acceptance of this fate as irreversible, he nonetheless, or perhaps precisely for this reason, attained a voice that was distinct among German writers of his time. It is characterized, above all, by its authenticity, which is vouched for not only by the enormous realities to which Améry gives witness, but also by the form his testimony finds in artistic expression. His prose is both forceful and elegant, hardened by the lessons of Auschwitz and tempered by irony, the latter a means by which he tacitly admitted, but also opposed, the onsets of actuality against his vulnerable person.

Améry's language is stamped by the clarity and verve of French, the main idiom of his daily life in exile, and by the complexities and flexibility of his native German, into which he freely infused Latinisms, Gallicisms, and turns of German speech that had become markedly quaint or outmoded. He skillfully balanced changes of perspective, tending to avoid, where possible, the first person pronoun as obtrusive or, as he sometimes felt, pretentious, taking recourse instead to the impersonal "one" or, more pointedly, to the third person "he." In later works, he sought even greater ironic distance from himself through use of a self-doubting, self-accusatory "you." Not least, the incessant reader Améry excelled at incorporating into his essays lines of verse, images, allusions, formulations, and turns of phrase from the vast store of German literature with which he was intimately familiar. In *At the Mind's Limits*, beside the clearly indicated quotations from Goethe, Hölderlin, Schnitzler, Kraus, and Thomas Mann, for example, there are still more, unmarked, from Schiller, Morgenstern, Brecht, Celan, and others. Améry employed this device with sovereign ease and without ostentation. It is the natural outgrowth of a lifetime spent, but for the violent interruption of the Nazi period, in close and affectionate association with literature.

Améry's decision not to revise *At the Mind's Limits* when, after eleven years, it appeared in a new edition, stemmed from his refusal to make any concessions to what he once called the "terror of current events." But he also confirmed, in a stock-taking two years before his death, that the world of his thought had been, and still was, one of "continual revision." Accordingly, in the face of the almost daily political murder that had become an affliction of the decade, he sharply qualified the approval he had expressed in his book, and elsewhere, for the act of counterviolence (under certain extreme conditions of human suffering), and condemned the phenomenon of international terrorism as sheer, arbitrary aggression, which sought to legitimize itself historically through a political apology. It was, in fact, clearly outspoken positions like this—which the unbending moralist Améry assumed also against the neo-Hegelians and the dialecticians of historical materialism—that led to his breach with the New Left, a movement with which he had not only sympathized but had believed himself to be actively united. This breach was widened still more by his absolute, although not uncritical, solidarity with the state of Israel. There was, in fact, no other intellectual on the German literary scene who defended Israel's existence as unequivocally and passionately as he did, again and again, in his books, in newspaper and magazine articles, in forums and discussions, particularly with students and other young people of the Left. Every threat to the Jewish state, which he visited for the first and only time in 1976, caused him alarm, and when, under the guise of anti-Zionism, he witnessed a re-emergence of antisemitism in Germany, he recognized that his book had lost none of its urgency. He expressly intended the new edition as a warning, especially to those segments of the young generation which in ideological errancy had begun to espouse the cause of Israel's destruction.

Améry's Jewishness or, more accurately, his identity as a Jew touched the core of his being. Despite his resolute efforts to clarify this identity, evidenced most incisively in the essay "On the Necessity and Impossibility of Being a Jew," he was at times misunderstood by Jewish intellectuals, writers, and also spiritual leaders, who contested his right to call himself a Jew. They did this not on grounds of religious law (which he, the unconditional agnostic, would have rejected anyway), but because of his inability to identify with Judaism in any other way except that of the Jewish Nazi victim. They were unable to comprehend why, after all, he found it impossible to acquire a Jewish heritage, although this had not been part of his formative years and had burst upon him only in 1933, in the demonically negative form of the Nazi death threat. Améry was pained by this rejection, just as he genuinely suffered from a Jewishness that had no positive determinants in tradition or culture. But he persisted in his Jewish identity, and, in the only way he could, he acted in consistency with it: as "a vehemently protesting Jew." This was his very personal distinction, and it is integral to any portrait of his existence.

The literary and journalistic tributes that followed upon the news of Améry's death were unanimous, and justly so, in viewing it in the context of his sternly introspective book on suicide, *Hand an sich legen. Diskurs über den Freitod* (1976). Aware that his health had been permanently impaired by every kind of adversity and want in the concentration camps, fearing the erosion of his intellectual powers (anticipated ten years earlier in his book on aging), he chose suicide as his personal protest, one both absurd and utopian, against the devastations of dying and the tyranny of a "natural" death. But perhaps it is not unwarranted to believe that still other experiences and convictions, which the commentators did not mention, strengthened Améry's resolve to tread this "last path to freedom," as he called it. Especially toward the end, he was downcast by increasing manifestations of a right-wing authoritarian restoration in German public life, along with the resurgence of antisemitism; his estrangement from the New Left, in whom his hopes had rested for a democratic Germany, had grown still more acute; the absorption of the Nazi past in its singularity and irreductibility into a universal theory of fascism and totalitarianism, something he had foreseen in *At the Mind's Limits*, but in a still somewhat removed future, was becoming reality before his eyes. The grotesqueness of the Maidanek trial in Düsseldorf, where the witnesses, survivors of the Nazi death camp, were subjected to derision by reactionary defense lawyers, filled him with bitterness. His response to the debate on the Statute of Limitations was a terse, poignant request not to the parliamentarians but to German society not to condemn the last remaining *victims* by morally exonerating their former torturers and thereby vindicating the atrocities. He was beset by a feeling that he was speaking into the wind, and this led to a despondent anger, growing resignation, and finally indifference. The close ties of friendship that still bound him to Germany, the readers there who awaited his word and esteemed it, his love for German literature, and his affection for the landscape were not enough to restrain him from silence.

In contemporary German intellectual life there is no voice that will replace his, and only the frail hope remains that its echoes will yet be heard.

Sidney Rosenfeld